The Most Inspiring World War 2 Stories

TRUE TALES OF BRAVERY, HOPE, AND TRIUMPH THAT EVERYONE SHOULD KNOW

BLOOMLIT PRESS

Copyright © 2025 by BloomLit Press

All rights reserved.

No part of this book may be reproduced in any form or by any electronic or mechanical means, including information storage and retrieval systems, without written permission from the author, except for the use of brief quotations in a book review.

Contents

Introduction   v

1. Dorie Miller at Pearl Harbor   1
2. Dunkirk   7
3. Nicholas Winton's Kindertransport   14
4. The Navajo Code Talkers   21
5. The Jedburghs   27
6. Witold Pilecki's Voluntary Imprisonment in Auschwitz   34
7. The Night Witches   43
8. The Tuskegee Airmen   49
9. Schindler's Jews   54
10. The Nisei Unit   61
11. Mad Jack Churchill   68
12. America's Most Decorated Soldier   75
13. The Sandakan Rescuers   82
14. The Battle of Britain   90
15. Glenn Miller and The Power of Music   98
16. The Ghost Army   105
17. John F. Kennedy and PT-109   111
18. The Siege of Bastogne   117
    Afterword   125
    Endnotes   127

Introduction

INTRODUCTION

By the late 1930s, tensions had begun to boil across Europe and Asia, inching the world toward a conflict unlike any before. In 1939, the war officially broke out, and over the next six years, it spread until nearly every corner of the globe felt its impact. In December 1941, an attack on Pearl Harbor drew the United States into the fight, expanding what was already a vast struggle. Entire nations were swept up in battles, and everyday life was replaced by hardship and uncertainty.

This clash tested the courage of millions—but it also revealed humanity's capacity for compassion in the face of danger. In these darkest moments, tales of bravery, friendship, and kindness shone through, reminding people that hope can flourish even when all seems lost.

This book highlights some of those remarkable stories, focusing on the human spirit and how everyday people chose to help one another, stand up for what was right, and remain steadfast in the face of fear.

Many have heard about the major battles and the most famous generals, but not everyone knows about lesser-known figures and extraordinary acts, such as Dorie Miller's bravery at Pearl Harbor or the 'Night Witches' of the Soviet Union.

As you read, you'll discover how individuals and communities navigated fear, overcame seemingly impossible obstacles, and demonstrated that hope and compassion can prevail even during wartime.

You're about to embark on a journey through history, meeting real heroes—some famous, many unknown—whose experiences will help you understand the far-reaching impact of World War II. Along the way, you'll find lessons to carry with you, lessons of strength, unity, and the enduring power of humanity.

Dorie Miller at Pearl Harbor

The morning sun had barely risen over Pearl Harbor, Hawaii, when a wave of Japanese planes roared into the bay on December 7, 1941. For many American sailors stationed there, it was a typical Sunday—time to relax or catch up on chores. But for one man named Doris "Dorie" Miller, a modest cook from Waco, Texas, that quiet morning would become a defining moment. Although he wasn't trained to use heavy weaponry, Dorie took heroic action that day and showed the world that courage can come from anywhere, regardless of rank, background, or race.

EARLY LIFE AND DREAMS

Born on October 12, 1919, Dorie Miller grew up on a farm in central Texas. He was known to friends and family as calm, hardworking, and physically strong. As a boy, he helped with chores, did odd jobs, and attended church on Sundays. In an era of strict racial segregation, opportunities for young African Americans were limited. Like many kids, Dorie dreamed of exploring the world, so when the chance came to join the U.S. Navy in 1939, he saw it as an escape from the fields of Texas—and a steady paycheck to support his family.

Yet, even within the Navy, African Americans were restricted to roles like mess attendants or cooks. At the time, the idea of black sailors handling weapons or commanding ships was practically unthinkable for many in military leadership. Still, Dorie adapted. He excelled in his duties in the kitchen and the mess hall, earning a reputation for reliability. Off duty, he sometimes practiced boxing—he was so strong and skillful that he became the ship's heavyweight champion aboard the USS West Virginia.

By late 1941, the USS West Virginia was moored in Pearl Harbor in Hawaii. The pacific islands felt like a paradise to many sailors, with its tropical breezes and beautiful scenery, yet there was an undercurrent of anxiety. The world was at war—fighting raged in Europe, while tensions built in the Pacific. Still, few on that base suspected a sudden attack on American soil.

That Sunday morning, Dorie had just finished serving breakfast. Above deck, some men were cleaning the ship, while others relaxed or wrote letters home. Many believed it would be a peaceful day. In a later interview, one of Miller's shipmates recalled, "We felt safe in Pearl Harbor. No one expected an assault here—until we heard the planes."

THE ATTACK BEGINS

Shortly before 8:00 AM, the first wave of Japanese bombers and fighters dived out of the clouds. Sirens blared, and bombs rained down on the harbor. Torpedoes streaked toward the battleships lined up like targets. Within moments, explosions shattered the morning calm. Smoke plumes rose into the sky as flames burned across decks.

Aboard the USS West Virginia, sailors scrambled to their battle stations. Dorie Miller, officially assigned to the mess hall, couldn't take on a combat role. Nonetheless, when the siren sounded, he rushed into action. He first attempted to help wounded crew members, carrying them to safer areas. According to accounts from surviving sailors, Miller disregarded the blasts around him, using his towering strength to lift injured comrades and move them away from burning wreckage.

As the attack intensified, many of the ship's gun crews had been taken out by the first strikes. One of the unmanned .50-caliber machine guns sat there, silent, while the skies above teemed with enemy planes. Miller's job in normal times was to serve meals and keep the dining areas clean, but at that moment, survival outweighed regulations! He'd never been officially trained on that gun, yet he saw it as the only chance to fight back...

Stepping behind the big machine gun, Dorie Miller began firing into the sky. The deafening roar of the weapon nearly drowned out the explosions around him. Shell casings clattered at his feet. He had no illusions of single-handedly stopping the entire attack, but he aimed carefully whenever a plane swooped close. Some shipmates later said they saw smoke trailing from at least one Japanese aircraft—possibly hit by Miller's burst of bullets.

Amid the chaos, he kept a cool head. One eyewitness recounted, "We couldn't believe a mess attendant was manning that gun like a pro. He looked calm, even when all heck was breaking loose."

Within minutes, the USS West Virginia was heavily damaged. Water rushed in through torpedo holes, and the deck was awash with flames. Sailors scrambled to abandon ship or fight fires. Dorie Miller continued to help the wounded, despite the risk of bombs and bullets. Eventually, the ship lurched and settled on the harbor floor, partially submerged.

When the attack ended, Pearl Harbor lay in ruins. Battleships like the USS Arizona were sunk outright; many others burned fiercely. Over 2,400 Americans lost their lives that morning. The United States was now fully drawn into World War II, a war raging across the globe for more than two years. Miller and the surviving crew of the West Virginia were taken ashore, where they learned the staggering toll of the assault.

RECOGNITION

Word of Dorie Miller's heroics soon spread. Despite his inexperience with machine guns, he fought back bravely and saved several shipmates from certain death. Some officers realized that, given the Navy's entrenched segregation policies, awarding an African American crewman for valor was unprecedented. However, in the face of such clear bravery, the top brass felt compelled to act.

In May 1942, Admiral Chester Nimitz, Commander in Chief of the U.S. Pacific Fleet, pinned the Navy Cross on Miller's chest, making him the first African American in the Navy to receive such a high honor. During the ceremony, Admiral Nimitz praised Miller's "extraordinary courage in the face of danger." The awarding of the Navy Cross sent a strong message that heroism knows no color barrier. For many black Americans, Dorie Miller became a symbol of hope and progress, proving their worth in a society that often denied them full rights.

Following his decorated service at Pearl Harbor, Miller traveled across the United States, participating in war bond rallies. Crowds gathered to see the quiet hero who had single-handedly taken on the enemy from a battered deck. In these public appearances, Miller spoke humbly, often giving credit to his fallen shipmates. He rarely boasted about his role.

Still, racism persisted. While a national hero on one hand, he remained limited to menial positions in the Navy. Eventually, he was assigned to another ship, the USS Liscome Bay, in the Pacific. Tragically, that ship was sunk by a Japanese submarine in November 1943, and Miller was reported missing in action.

The story of Dorie Miller did not end with the USS Liscome Bay. As the war continued, calls for equality in the armed forces grew louder. Advocates pointed to Miller's example: if he was brave enough to fight and give his life, why should any African American be denied the chance to serve in full combat roles or earn promotions? Eventually, in 1948, President Harry Truman ordered the desegregation of the U.S. military, marking a key milestone in the broader civil rights movement.

To this day, people honor Dorie Miller's memory, whether by naming a building or a naval ship in his honor, or by recounting his tale to teach young people about the true meaning of bravery and respect. His story proves that others' assumptions should limit no one. A cook can be a hero, and a closed door can be opened through courage.

As the United States mobilized for a war that stretched across oceans, small sparks of boldness lit the way. Dorie Miller's spark shone especially bright. By standing at a machine gun he never formally trained on, saving wounded friends, and bravely confronting an overwhelming assault, he turned a moment of tragedy into a legacy of hope. Countless Americans—both then and now—draw strength from his example, believing that in times of crisis, one person's action can inspire a whole nation. His bravery ensured that future generations would see beyond prejudice, realizing that talent, patriotism, and gallantry know no racial bounds. Indeed, Dorie Miller's heroism changed hearts, gave momentum to a broader fight for civil rights, and left a timeless lesson: courage is colorblind.

Dunkirk

In May 1940, a sleepy French town called Dunkirk suddenly became the center of a dramatic rescue that would change the course of World War II. Allied soldiers—mainly British, but also French and Belgian—found themselves trapped by fast-moving German troops. With their backs to the sea, they seemed doomed to either surrender or lose their lives. Yet, in what many called "a miracle," everyday people banded together to pull off one of the most astonishing mass evacuations in history. Known as Operation Dynamo, it involved a seemingly slapdash flotilla of navy ships, civilian fishing boats, and personal yachts racing across the English Channel to bring stranded soldiers home.

THE GATHERING STORM

The war in Europe erupted in September 1939. By the spring of 1940, German forces had swept through Belgium and northern France with alarming speed, using a military tactic called "blitzkrieg," which means "lightning war" in English. The Allies were caught off guard and found themselves badly outmaneuvered.

Within weeks, hundreds of thousands of British and Allied troops were pushed back to the Northern French coast. The beaches of Dunkirk became their last refuge. Supplies were scarce, morale was low, and the German army closed in. One British soldier, Private Kenneth Thomas, later wrote in a letter, "Each morning we woke up hoping for a miracle. Surrounded on land, the only hope was the sea."

The soldiers dug in along the coast, forming defensive lines. Meanwhile, British leaders in London, including Prime Minister Winston Churchill, scrambled for options. If the entire British Expeditionary Force was captured or destroyed, the war might effectively be over for Britain, leaving Germany as the unchallenged ruler of Western Europe.

CORNERED AT THE BEACH

By May 26, over 400,000 Allied soldiers huddled on the Dunkirk beaches or in the rubble of the surrounding town. The cold waters of the English Channel offered the only possible escape route. Yet, the harbor was shallow and partially blocked by damaged ships. Large Royal Navy vessels risked air attacks from German planes as soon as they approached.

Bombs dropped from the sky daily. Artillery shells shook the ground. Soldiers tried to keep their spirits up, but the atmosphere felt grim. They formed long queues in the sand, waiting for small boats to ferry them to larger ships offshore. The threat of air raids was constant. Each day, columns of black smoke from burning vehicles and warehouses rose into the sky.

Lance Corporal Sheila Clarke, a nurse on a medical transport, described the scene, "Men queued in perfect lines, even when bombs fell close by. It showed their discipline—but also their desperation to leave."

Back in Britain, the Admiralty (in charge of the Royal Navy) devised a bold plan called Operation Dynamo. They needed to rescue as many soldiers as possible, knowing German tanks could roll into Dunkirk at any moment. But the Royal Navy alone couldn't do it quickly enough. So they called on everyone who owned a seaworthy vessel—fishing boats, pleasure cruisers, ferries, barges, even small lifeboats.

A wave of volunteers came forward. Some were retired sailors, others were weekend boaters who'd never ventured far from shore. They bravely set out, crossing the rough Channel, determined to do their part. One fisherman, George Atkins, explained his decision: "These were our boys, our brothers. If my little boat could bring even one home safely, I had to go."

This ragtag fleet, later nicknamed the "Little Ships of Dunkirk," became essential to shuttling soldiers from the beaches onto larger destroyers or directly back to England.

BRAVING THE CHANNEL

On May 27, Operation Dynamo officially began. The first wave of ships, large and small, left British shores. Many of the civilian captains had no experience piloting under combat conditions, nor did they have any illusions about the dangers of German dive-bombers and U-boats lurking beneath the water.

Private Leonard Davies, one of the first rescued from the beach, later recounted, "Seeing a row of tiny vessels bobbing on the horizon felt surreal. They were like angels sailing toward us in a nightmare."

During daylight, the German Luftwaffe (air force) swooped down, dropping bombs and strafing the overloaded boats. At night, searchlights and flares lit the sky. Yet the rescue continued day after day. Sometimes, the Little Ships had to wait offshore, forming makeshift piers or tying themselves together so that soldiers could hop from one boat to another. The beaches themselves, littered with abandoned vehicles and supplies, became a zone of chaos and noise.

As the days passed, Allied troops on the beach faced a terrifying ordeal. Some stood knee-deep in the surf for hours, feeling the chilly waves wash over them, hoping their turn to board would come soon. Others crouched behind sand dunes, listening nervously for the sound of approaching tanks. Many had not eaten a proper meal for days. They were exhausted and haunted by the fear that the evacuation might fail.

And yet, a spirit of camaraderie prevailed. Soldiers helped one another stay afloat if a bomb blast caused them to stumble. Officers reassured their men by telling them about the thousands who had already escaped. The coastline was a scene of both terror and solidarity. Each boat's arrival felt like a lifeline, a chance to stay alive.

Throughout the operation, many heroic moments took place. Royal Navy destroyers sailed dangerously close to shore to embark troops faster. Some were sunk by air attacks, others limped back to England with massive damage. Meanwhile, small boat captains rescued men from sinking ships even as bombs rained down around them.

French and Belgian forces fought on the outskirts of Dunkirk, buying time for the evacuations. Though overshadowed by the spotlight on British soldiers, these Allied troops fought desperately to hold off the German advance. A French officer, Captain Henri Renaud, described it as follows: "We knew we'd likely be captured, but every hour we held the line meant more men escaped. That was our duty."

Many soldiers who reached the safety of a ship found themselves comforting the wounded or the traumatized. Some tried to keep morale high with jokes, others simply stared into space, trying to process the shock of battle.

By June 3, a staggering number of Allied soldiers—over 300,000—had been evacuated. News of this "Miracle of Dunkirk" spread quickly. Though the British Army left behind heavy equipment, tanks, and supplies, at least the core of its manpower lived to fight another day. On June 4, Winston Churchill addressed the House of Commons, praising the bravery of everyone involved but also cautioning that wars aren't won by evacuations alone. In his famous speech, he vowed, "We shall fight on the beaches... we shall never surrender."

Churchill's words resonated with a British public who had feared a much worse outcome. They realized how close they came to seeing an entire army wiped out. The safe return of so many soldiers became a rallying cry, boosting morale and uniting the country's resolve.

EVERYDAY PEOPLE TO THE RESCUE

Countless everyday people brought their boats across. Among them was Charles Lightoller, a former Titanic officer who skippered the yacht *Sundowner*, carrying over a hundred men in a vessel built for much fewer. Another was Nick Carter, a barge operator who calmly ferried dozens of troops at a time. Carter remembered, "Their eyes looked hollow from exhaustion, but when they saw us, they smiled like we were a grand navy."

One fisherman used a small open boat to rescue men who clung to a capsized landing craft. He made multiple trips in the face of strafing planes. A teenage boy accompanied his father, taking the wheel while his dad helped haul soldiers aboard. These tales highlight how entire families and communities risked everything to save strangers across the Channel.

At first, Dunkirk might not seem like a victory. The Allies had been driven back, leaving the French coast in German hands. Yet the survival of over 300,000 Allied troops—especially the bulk of Britain's professional army—allowed the fight against Nazi Germany to continue. Had these men been captured, Britain's ability to defend itself would have crumbled.

The Dunkirk evacuation became a symbol of determination and the strength of unity. It demonstrated how, even when all seems lost, teamwork and perseverance can transform a disaster into a kind of triumph. This spirit, sometimes called the "Dunkirk Spirit," carried Britain through the dark months of the Blitz and beyond.

It also inspired other occupied nations, showing them that not all was hopeless. If a haphazard flotilla could rescue an entire army, perhaps there *was* still room for miraculous turns of fate. The British government used newsreels of the evacuation, along with Churchill's stirring speeches, to boost morale and rally the population for the brutal battles yet to come.

What makes Dunkirk so inspiring? Perhaps it's the recognition that ordinary folks—fishermen, weekend sailors, barge operators—proved as vital as any soldier. They showed that an entire nation's willpower could move mountains (or, in this case, rescue an entire army). Dunkirk also taught that you don't have to be a general or a prime minister to make a difference. A single boat, loaded with determination, can play its part in shaping history.

We may never again see a flotilla of tiny boats save an army. Still, that image endures—an armada of battered craft cutting through the waves, forging hope out of despair. Dunkirk stands tall among World War II's most inspiring tales because it wasn't a retreat; it was a testament to the power of people coming together, refusing to abandon one another when it mattered most.

Nicholas Winton's Kindertransport

In the spring of 1939, the city of Prague was filled with worry. Nazi Germany had marched into Czechoslovakia, and many Jewish families feared for their lives. For them, it felt as though a dark cloud hung low, bringing threats of persecution and violence. In that tense atmosphere, a young British stockbroker named Nicholas Winton unexpectedly stepped forward to help. Almost by accident, he stumbled upon the dire situation that hundreds of Jewish children faced under Nazi rule—and, acting quickly, he organized what would become one of the most remarkable rescue efforts of World War II: The Kindertransport.

BRIEFCASE HERO

In December 1938, Nicholas Winton was preparing for a skiing holiday in Switzerland. Instead, a friend urged him to come to Prague to see the refugee camps for Jews forced from the Sudetenland by Nazi forces. Astonished by the misery he encountered, Winton realized these children were in grave danger. Many countries had imposed strict immigration rules, making it nearly impossible for Jewish families to flee. Winton sensed that time was running short—if he did nothing, many of these children would be trapped. He set up a makeshift office in a hotel room in central Prague, writing letters to governments, charities, and anyone who might help. He hoped to whisk children out of Czechoslovakia to safety in Britain, even though he wasn't part of any official agency. Talking about those first hectic days, Winton later admitted, "I wasn't looking to be a hero. I just saw kids who needed rescuing and realized I was in a position to do something."

Simply wanting to help wasn't enough; the project needed official documents, travel permits, and funding. Families would often line up in Winton's cramped workspace, desperately seeking a spot for their children. Their faces reflected both hope and heartbreak—they understood they might never see their little ones again if war erupted. Nevertheless, handing a child to a stranger seemed safer than leaving them in a hostile environment.

Back in London, Winton asked acquaintances to sponsor these children and pay a 50-pound guarantee required by British immigration authorities (a substantial sum at the time). He also arranged for foster families across England to host them. Along with a small circle of volunteers, he navigated endless paperwork. Tina, a teenage helper, later recalled, "We wrote letters day and night. For each child, there were forms to fill out, photos to attach. Nicholas insisted every detail be perfect."

The Kindertransport missions typically used trains to move these children out of Czechoslovakia and across Germany to ports where they would board ships bound for England. Each departure brought a flurry of tears, relief, and frantic goodbyes. Because many parents couldn't leave, they stood on the platform, waving until the train was out of sight. Some children were just toddlers, holding tags with their names pinned to their coats. One evacuee, Eva Weiss, recalled in her later years, "I was only seven. My mother told me to be brave, that I was going to a place where I'd be safe. I remember the whistle of the train—it sounded like a promise and a heartbreak all at once."

For those kids, the journey involved passing through territory under Nazi control, risking searches at border checkpoints. They traveled in locked train cars for days, sustained by limited food and comforted by volunteer escorts. Whenever an officer would come aboard, everyone held their breath, fearing an official might decide to turn them back.

Nicholas Winton juggled his normal job in London's financial district with the Kindertransport rescue efforts. By day, he'd sit at his desk handling stock transactions; by evening, he was writing letters to potential foster families or finalizing the logistics for the next train. He usually signed off documents under an organization name he invented, the "British Committee for Refugees from Czechoslovakia (Children's Section)," giving his efforts a sense of formality. In reality, it was mostly just Winton and a few dedicated helpers.

Though the British government provided grudging support, it was never as simple as he hoped. Finding enough host families was a constant challenge. Some children needed medical care; others spoke no English. Nonetheless, Winton pressed on, convinced that saving even one life was worth every ounce of frustration. "It's not about grand gestures," he once said. "It's about doing what you can, with what you have, where you are."

By late August 1939, tensions across Europe were at a boiling point. Hitler's Germany was poised to invade Poland, and it was clear that war was imminent. Winton arranged his largest Kindertransport train yet—about 250 children on a single departure. It was scheduled to leave Prague on September 1, 1939. That very morning, Germany attacked Poland, and Europe was hurled into World War II. Borders slammed shut. The train never departed. Those children disappeared into the chaos, leaving Winton haunted by their fate. Still, during the months before the war, Winton's network had managed to evacuate over 600 kids. Each now lived in safety with families across England. Although heartbreak lingered for the ones left behind, for many families, a second chance was created. One of those saved children, Marie Rosen, would grow up to become a teacher in the UK. She wrote in her memoir, "I owe my life to the chance Nicholas Winton gave me. I sometimes wonder who I would've been without him. Perhaps no one at all."

A NEW LIFE

For the children who made it to England, the experiences varied. Some found warm, welcoming foster families that treated them like their own. Others struggled with language barriers and missed their parents desperately. A few faced unkind guardians or teasing from local classmates. Despite the challenges, though, they were safe. Their biggest worry was adapting to an unfamiliar culture, rather than hiding from armed patrols or the threat of deportation to concentration camps. Support groups formed to help these new arrivals. Winton and other volunteers stayed in touch, ensuring kids were monitored, schooled, and offered a sense of community. Over time, these children, known as "Winton's Children," formed lasting friendships, bound by the shared memory of rescue. Many learned English quickly, excelled in academics or music, and grew up to become scientists, artists, teachers, and business leaders.

For decades after the war, Nicholas Winton remained surprisingly modest. He rarely spoke publicly about his role in saving these children. Even some close friends had little clue about his past heroics. It wasn't until 1988, nearly fifty years later, that his wife discovered a scrapbook in the attic—packed with photographs, letters, and lists of the rescued kids. She shared it with a BBC television program, leading to a dramatic on-air reunion between Winton and several of "his" children.

During that televised moment, the now-grown evacuees sat in the audience, many with families of their own. When the host asked anyone saved by Winton to stand, nearly the entire audience rose. Winton, visibly moved, realized his quiet efforts had blossomed into countless lives. It's estimated that today there are over 6,000 descendants of the kids Winton helped rescue. One of them, Vera Diamant, declared, "He gave us a future we never imagined. I discovered that hope can arrive even when darkness seems total."

Want to see true gratitude in action? *Scan this QR code and watch the heartwarming reunion of Nicholas Winton with the children he rescued—40 years after his heroic Kindertransport mission.*

What stands out most about the Kindertransport is how a single individual, without official authority, changed so many lives. Nicholas Winton used a kitchen-table office approach—writing letters, organizing foster placements, and persuading authorities—yet he managed to create a rescue pipeline. Many have compared him to others who saved Jews during the war, such as Oskar Schindler who we'll talk about in Chapter 9.

Today, the rescued children—some well into their later years—often refer to themselves as "Nicky's Children." They tell stories of arriving in Britain, holding onto a single suitcase, sometimes clutching a favorite doll or a photograph of their parents. They explain how they adapted to new families and discovered the English language. Many, upon learning the true scope of Winton's efforts, felt deep gratitude. Others continued to raise awareness about the Holocaust and the dangers of hatred and discrimination.

Their legacy resonates in schools and museums, inspiring new generations to ask: "How can I help when I see injustice?" The example they point to is Nicholas Winton, who didn't wait for permission—he stepped in as soon as he realized the urgency of the situation.

Nicholas Winton lived to see the fruits of his kindness. He passed away in 2015, at the age of 106, praised worldwide as a symbol of selfless service. Many recognized him as a man who refused to do nothing in the face of evil. His path wasn't free of obstacles—he encountered plenty of bureaucratic red tape and narrow thinking—but he pressed on regardless.

For kids today, his story highlights how one person's dedication can transform lives. You don't have to wear a uniform or hold an official title to do what's right. When asked if he felt proud, Winton often shrugged, "We are all capable of more than we think. Sometimes you simply must step forward because no one else will."

That quiet determination speaks volumes. He didn't rely on grand gestures or big speeches—just consistent work, compassion, and a willingness to break rules that kept children in danger.

The Navajo Code Talkers

In the thick of World War II, while tanks rumbled across Europe and warships clashed in the Pacific, a group of young Native American men stepped forward with a skill only they possessed: a unique language that nobody outside their community truly understood. They were the Navajo Code Talkers, members of the Navajo Nation who used their complex, unwritten language to create an unbreakable code. Long after the war, their contribution was finally recognized, but at the time, their work was top secret—so secret, in fact, that even their families didn't know the details! Today, their story stands out as one of the most inspiring tales of ingenuity, courage, and patriotism in WWII.

TRAINING IN SECRET

By 1942, the United States had fully joined the war, battling in both Europe and the Pacific. The fighting against the Japanese stretched across vast oceans, from the islands of Guadalcanal to the beaches of Iwo Jima. U.S. Marine units needed a secure way to communicate their plans, especially since Japanese intelligence agents were skilled codebreakers. Repeatedly, American messages were intercepted, and soldiers' lives were put at risk.

At the same time, recruiters in the southwestern United States noticed something special. The Navajo language was incredibly tough for outsiders to learn—an unwritten, tonal language with no direct translation for many English terms. A few officials hypothesized that Navajo could become the perfect building block for a military code. So, the Marines began seeking Navajo men who were willing to enlist and put their language to use. One of the first to sign up was Chester Nez, who later recalled, "When they told me they wanted to use my language to help defeat the enemy, I felt proud. It was a chance to serve my country and my people."

About 29 Navajo men were initially recruited and sent to Camp Pendleton in California. Once there, they underwent the same grueling Marine Corps basic training as everyone else—obstacle courses, drills, and marksmanship. But after hours, they gathered in small huts and invented a code based on their language. They had to adapt Navajo words to represent military vocabulary that didn't exist in everyday life. For example, they used the Navajo word for "turtle" to refer to a tank, or "silver oak leaf" to describe a rank insignia.

In some cases, they spelled out words letter by letter, using Navajo words that started with certain letters of the English alphabet. The code had multiple layers—meaning if anyone intercepted it, even if they spoke Navajo, they wouldn't automatically understand the message. It took weeks of brainstorming and practice. A sign in their workspace warned them not to speak about what they were doing. They even had to burn their notes at the end of each day. John Brown Jr., one of the code creators, remembered, "We locked ourselves in rooms, tested each other, refining the words. We knew it had to be fast and flawless if it was going to work."

HITTING THE FRONT LINES

After the code took shape, the Navajo men were shipped off to the Pacific, where the Marines faced fierce Japanese resistance. Their first big test came during battles like Guadalcanal and Tarawa. Fighting in steamy jungles and across coral reefs, the Marines needed to coordinate artillery strikes and ground attacks swiftly. Radio transmissions had to be quick yet accurate.

Navajo Code Talkers carried bulky radios, often dashing through gunfire to reach vantage points. They'd crouch in foxholes, spinning the radio dial to the right frequency, and bark out orders in Navajo code. A typical message might sound like a conversation about animals, family, or natural elements. But in reality, it spelled out vital info—enemy locations, how many troops were attacking, or what supplies were needed. The difference was that nobody, not even the best code-breakers on the enemy side, could understand it. Louis Camacho, who saw action on many islands, recalled one instance, "We were pinned down by snipers. The major needed artillery on a specific ridge. I sent the coordinates in Navajo code, and within minutes, the shells landed exactly where we needed them."

Being a Code Talker was extremely dangerous. Japanese troops quickly learned that Navajo radio operators were passing critical information. If a sniper spotted a man with a radio, that soldier became a prime target. So, Code Talkers had to stay constantly on the move. They also worried about being mistaken for the enemy since they stood out physically and didn't speak English over the radio. Sometimes, they traveled with bodyguards who were under orders to protect them—and, in grim scenarios, never let them be captured alive.

The conditions were harsh: blazing island heat, mosquitoes, rotting jungle terrain. The men ate ration packs and slept in foxholes, if they slept at all. Because messages had to be decoded and transmitted quickly, Code Talkers often worked around the clock, their radio sets whirring through the night. Despite it all, their morale stayed high, partly because they believed so deeply in their role. They knew how essential their coded words were for saving Allied lives.

As the war progressed, Code Talkers found themselves in nearly every major Pacific battle. Some of the toughest fighting occurred on Saipan, where American forces needed to gain a foothold in the Mariana Islands. Japanese defenders put up fierce resistance. Once again, the Navajo code proved invaluable for coordinating complicated maneuvers under heavy fire.

However, perhaps the most famous instance was the Battle of Iwo Jima in early 1945. The rocky, ash-covered island bristled with Japanese tunnels and bunkers. When the Marines landed, the fighting turned brutal, with thousands of casualties on both sides. The Code Talkers worked day and night, relaying everything from target coordinates for naval gunfire to simple status updates on casualties. They stayed calm while shells exploded around them. Their speed and accuracy made a crucial difference. One Marine officer credited a team of Code Talkers with saving countless lives by directing artillery onto a hidden enemy battery. In a letter to his superiors, he wrote, "Were it not for the Navajo code and the men who transmitted it, our losses would have been far greater. Their contribution cannot be overstated."

During the entire Pacific campaign, the Navajo code was never cracked. Japanese intelligence experts couldn't unravel its secrets. This success stemmed from the language's complexity and the Code Talkers' sheer discipline. They memorized hundreds of code terms, never mixing them up. The code's speed also mattered. An encoded message that might take half an hour to decipher by machine could be sent and understood by a trained Navajo in seconds. That speed offered a massive tactical edge in battles where every second counted. This unstoppable code gave the Marines a sense of confidence. They knew that if they needed to regroup or call for reinforcements, the enemy wouldn't figure out their plans. In a war known for intense island-hopping campaigns, that advantage was worth its weight in gold.

When WWII ended in 1945, many Code Talkers simply returned to their Navajo reservations or tried to find work in nearby towns. They were not greeted with the same fanfare as some other veterans. Their mission remained classified, meaning they weren't allowed to talk openly about what they did. Even family members didn't know the full story. Some men carried on with their lives, working as farmers, ranchers, or in city jobs, quietly harboring the knowledge that they had played a significant part in history. But the code's success didn't go entirely unnoticed. Officers who had witnessed it recognized the Code Talkers' skill and commitment. It just took time—decades, actually—for the U.S. government to publicly acknowledge their achievements. In 1968, the code was finally declassified, allowing the veterans to share their experiences.

LEGACY

In 1982, President Ronald Reagan declared August 14 as Navajo Code Talkers Day, a tribute that has since expanded to honor all Code Talkers from various tribes who served in WWII. Museums, documentaries, and books gradually brought their story to a wider audience. Later, in 2001, the surviving Code Talkers were awarded the Congressional Gold Medal.

Today, their families carry forward the memory of these men's sacrifices. The code they invented stands as a testament to brilliant teamwork and cultural pride. At the unveiling of a Code Talker monument, one of the veterans softly said, "It was our language that helped win the war. I hope young people realize their heritage can do amazing things if used for the greater good."

The Navajo Code Talkers illustrate how even a seemingly small or marginalized community can have an outsized influence. Each coded radio message was a lifeline, each syllable a shield against enemy eavesdropping. They turned their mother tongue into a formidable secret weapon—one that remained uncracked and unstoppable. They also showed that the voices of Indigenous people—voices often overlooked—could save thousands of lives and forge a legacy that outlasts us all.

The Jedburghs

On a dark, moonless night in June 1944, high above the countryside of France, a small plane flew silently. Inside it sat three men, each from a different nationality. They wore heavy gear and parachutes and could feel their hearts pounding. The pilot nodded, and a green light flashed. In an instant, these three leaped into the night sky, trusting their parachutes to carry them safely to the ground. This was Operation Jedburgh.

Operation Jedburgh was a secret plan created by the Allies during the war. The purpose of this mission was simple but very dangerous: small teams of three would parachute into places that were under Nazi control. Once on the ground, they would team up with local Resistance fighters to fight back from within. These special teams took their name, "Jedburgh," from a town in Scotland. Nobody is exactly sure why that name was chosen, but it added to the mystery and secrecy of the mission. Each three-person team usually had:

- An American or British officer (experienced in military leadership or sabotage).
- A local officer (often French) to communicate with citizens.
- A radio operator (someone who could send messages back to Allied commanders).

These teams were incredibly brave. If the Nazis ever captured them, they would have likely faced a horrible future. Yet, the Jedburghs knew the risk and still jumped straight into enemy territory. Their mission was to stir hope among people who were forced to live under Nazi rule—and, of course, to cause trouble for the German army.

TRAINING FOR THE UNTHINKABLE

Before they jumped into action, Jedburgh members needed some of the most demanding training imaginable. They practiced parachuting at night, landing on rough farmland or in thick forests. They studied how to set explosives, use different weapons, and send secret radio messages using Morse code. They also learned to live off the land in case they had to hide from enemy patrols for days or weeks at a time. "Our training was both mental and physical. We had to be ready for anything—fighting, making friends with local villagers, and even cooking up clever plans to fool the enemy." Colonel Aaron Bank, one of the American Jedburgh officers, recalled.

This training took place in secret bases across England. Many regular soldiers had no idea the Jedburghs existed. The program was so top-secret that new Jedburgh members were warned not to tell anyone, even their families, precisely what they were learning or where they were headed.

A LEAP INTO THE UNKNOWN

On June 6, 1944—also known as D-Day—the Allies landed on the beaches of Normandy, France. This was a huge invasion meant to push the Nazis out of France. But the Allies knew they would need extra help. The Nazis had strong defenses, and they could send in additional troops by train and truck. That's where the Jedburghs came in.

Right after D-Day, small planes carried Jedburgh teams high above the French countryside. "The hush before the jump was eerie. We all knew we might land in a field full of enemies—or we might land in a friendly farmyard. We prayed for the best." Major Clifford Wingate, a British Jedburgh, wrote in his diary,

When the pilot gave the signal, the Jedburghs jumped into the cold, black sky, trusting their parachutes to guide them safely. Most of the time, they landed far from any towns, so they had to hide their chutes immediately and find the local Resistance groups before daylight gave them away.

Finding the local Resistance fighters was never easy. Sometimes, the teams landed in precisely the right spot, and villagers were waiting for them. More often, the Jedburghs had to trek through forests or fields, guided by starlight. Local farmers or townspeople would whisper code words or phrases to the Jedburghs to ensure they were talking to the right people. Everybody was afraid of spies. "We had to be careful with every word. A wrong phrase or a wrong face could mean capture." One French Jedburgh, Captain Roger Warin, remembered. But once the Jedburghs met up with the Resistance, they formed fast friendships. The Resistance fighters had been risking their lives to sabotage Nazi roads, railways, and communication lines. With the Jedburghs' help, they received more weapons, training, and crucial radio contact with Allied leaders back in Britain.

RADIO LIFELINES

Why were radios so important? Because they allowed the Jedburgh teams to send secret messages about what was happening on the ground. For example, they might tap a message in Morse code: "Enemy train moving south. Send explosives." Within a few nights, Allied airplanes might drop crates of supplies—like guns, ammo, and medicine—by parachute into a remote field.

These radio transmissions had to be short because the Nazis were always listening for enemy radio signals. If they detected a signal for too long, they could track it and send soldiers to catch the Jedburghs. So radio operators became experts at working quickly. Sergeant William "Bill" Colby, an American radio operator, said, "We learned to set up, send a coded message, and pack away in under ten minutes. Any longer, and we might have uninvited guests knocking at the door."

While the radio operators sent messages, other Jedburgh members focused on training the Resistance in acts of sabotage. Blowing up bridges and train tracks was a common task. If the Nazis couldn't move troops or supplies easily, they'd have trouble stopping the Allied advance. One British soldier, Lieutenant John Singlaub, described one such mission, "We crept along an old railway line late at night, planting explosives where the track curved. By morning, part of the track was gone, and a Nazi train lay tilted, unable to move. Every bit of confusion we caused gave the Allies an edge."

These sabotage missions were usually quick and had to be done in secret. Sometimes, the Resistance and Jedburghs also carried out ambushes on small Nazi patrols. Each success gave more confidence to ordinary French people, who began to realize that help was truly there for them.

Along with the danger came many moments of kindness and solidarity. The Jedburghs and the Resistance fighters often stayed in farmhouses, barns, or even hidden cellars offered by local families. These families shared whatever they had to eat—even if it was just bread, cheese, and soup. In return, the Jedburghs brought news about the outside world, letting people know that the Allied armies were fighting their way through France.

In many towns, people began to call the Jedburghs "the ghosts" because they appeared, helped with an operation, and vanished again into the countryside. A French villager whose family once sheltered a Jedburgh team said, "They showed up like angels in the middle of the night, bringing hope and reminding us that we were not alone." As the

Allies pushed inland from the beaches of Normandy, the Nazis tried to send reinforcements to stop them. But because of the Jedburgh teams and the Resistance, many roads and railways were damaged or destroyed. This slowed the Nazis down. They had to split their forces to chase the Resistance fighters, leaving fewer troops to face the main Allied invasion force.

Operation Jedburgh was only one part of a massive effort by many brave groups, but historians agree that these small teams made a big difference. By August 1944, Allied troops were able to liberate Paris, greeted by cheering crowds. The Nazis were forced to retreat on multiple fronts. Every bridge blown up or train derailed helped the Allies gain ground and end the war sooner. Not every story ended happily. Some Jedburgh teams were discovered by Nazi patrols and captured. Others lost men during fierce gunfights. Yet, their sacrifices were not wasted. Each fallen member inspired others to carry on. Major Fred Milton, a survivor of one Jedburgh mission, later said, "We lost good friends out there, but we knew our work would free entire towns. When you see people celebrate their freedom, you realize any risk was worth it." The courage of the Jedburgh teams also influenced the future. After the war, some Jedburgh veterans became leaders in their countries. Others used their experience to develop new kinds of special operations. The lessons they learned—how to coordinate with local fighters, how to organize secret missions, and how to adapt quickly—still guide modern special forces around the world.

One of the most amazing things about Operation Jedburgh was the mix of nationalities and backgrounds. Americans, British, French, Dutch, Belgian—they worked together in tiny teams, sharing whatever they had. They ate together, slept in the same hiding spots, and faced the same dangers. Their mission depended on trust. They had to trust each other and trust the local people they fought beside.

A GIANT IMPACT FROM SMALL TEAMS

Operation Jedburgh proves that small groups can change big events. You might wonder: Could just three people and a radio make a difference in a war that involved millions of soldiers? The answer is yes. Because those three people were never really alone, they teamed up with hundreds of local Resistance fighters, and each mission weakened the Nazi grip on France a little more.

Operation Jedburgh shone a light in dark times. These brave men didn't just drop into enemy territory to blow things up. They also inspired ordinary people—farmers, teachers, shopkeepers—to stand up against the Nazis. They showed everyone that no matter how strong an enemy seems, if people work together with courage, they can bring change. "We were small in number, but we carried the flame of hope. We aimed to pass that flame to the oppressed so they could light their own way to freedom," Jedburgh Colonel Aaron Bank said. That flame spread. Town after town discovered that they weren't alone. They had help from the skies, from new friends who brought weapons, and a determination to see France freed from Nazi rule.

By forcing the Nazis to fight on multiple fronts—battling both Allied armies and hidden Resistance fighters—Germany's defeat came sooner. In doing so, the Jedburghs spared countless civilians in occupied countries from prolonged suffering and helped villages across France gain their freedom more quickly than anyone had anticipated.

Witold Pilecki's Voluntary Imprisonment in Auschwitz

In the early days of World War II, Poland faced terrible hardships. Nazi Germany had invaded the country, forcing countless people into harsh living conditions and terrorizing anyone who dared resist. Amid this chaos, a Polish army officer named Witold Pilecki came up with a very bold—some would say shocking—plan. He decided that if the world was going to learn the truth about the Nazis' most terrifying prison camp, he would have to see it himself and report back. The place was called Auschwitz.

Growing up, Witold Pilecki was known for being polite, caring, and determined. He came from a patriotic Polish family, and he valued honor and loyalty above all else. When Nazi Germany and the Soviet Union sliced up Poland in 1939, Pilecki joined the underground resistance—sometimes called the Home Army—to fight back in secret. Soon, the Polish Resistance began hearing horrifying rumors about Auschwitz: families disappearing, terrible conditions, and unimaginable cruelty. Yet there was little evidence. Many people outside Poland didn't fully believe how dreadful things had become. That's when Pilecki proposed something extraordinary: "I will go in, see it for myself, and get the facts out to the world."

ENTERING THE GATES OF HELL

In September 1940, Witold Pilecki put his plan into action. He deliberately allowed himself to be caught in a Nazi roundup in Warsaw. When the guards grabbed him along with other civilians, nobody guessed he had chosen this path on purpose. After a few frightening days, he was sent by train to Auschwitz, the sprawling camp in southern Poland.

Those who arrived at Auschwitz typically had their belongings stolen and their hair shaved. They were given striped uniforms, a prisoner number, and were forced into overcrowded barracks. Guards shouted orders constantly, and guard dogs barked at the slightest movement. The heavy stench of fear hung in the air. Many who were sent there felt as if all hope had been stripped away.

But Pilecki held onto his secret mission. He wanted to form a small underground network inside the camp, gather information about the atrocities, and somehow smuggle that information out to the Polish Resistance. "I felt the eyes of the world upon me," he would later write in his report. "I knew if I failed, no one would know the truth."

From the moment Pilecki stepped through the gates, he knew survival would be challenging. Prisoners slept on hard wooden shelves, often with very little food. They woke up before sunrise to stand outside for roll call, no matter the weather. Brutal guards struck anyone who seemed too slow or too weak. People from many backgrounds—Jews, Poles, political prisoners, and others—were all crammed together under the watchful eye of the SS (the Nazi guards).

Still, Pilecki never let despair consume him. He quietly made friends, earning trust by sharing what tiny bits of food he could spare and by listening to people's stories. In hushed voices at night, he gathered names, details, and descriptions of the camp's brutalities. A fellow inmate later said of Pilecki, "He looked at you with calm eyes, and in that look, you felt that maybe not all was lost." Over time, Pilecki's small band of allies formed. They found secret ways to meet, even though the risk was enormous. If any Nazi guard discovered what they were doing, they would face terrible punishment. Yet these men believed that letting the outside world know what was happening was worth every danger they faced.

BUILDING A SECRET RESISTANCE

Inside Auschwitz, Pilecki began organizing a quiet resistance group. Its goals were threefold:

- Help prisoners survive by sharing extra clothing, food, or medicine.
- Gather evidence of Nazi crimes—write down names of murdered prisoners, record descriptions of forced labor, and detail every act of cruelty.
- Send messages to the outside world and ask for help—or possibly plan a larger prisoner uprising if the chance arose.

They used code names, whispered in corners, and wrote secret notes in ways the guards wouldn't detect. One of Pilecki's allies described these nighttime gatherings as a "glimmer of hope in the darkest place on Earth." Every shred of information they gathered—no matter how small—could make a difference. Meanwhile, people kept arriving at Auschwitz from all over Europe, increasing the flow of horrifying stories. Jews, Polish political prisoners, Roma families, and others were forced into labor, starved, or worse. Pilecki's heart grew heavier every day as he realized the scale of what the Nazis were doing. Yet he refused to give up, often repeating to himself a simple motto: "I am here to bear witness."

One of the greatest challenges Pilecki faced was getting his findings out of the camp. There was no easy way to send letters. Guards searched prisoners constantly. Anyone caught communicating with the outside world faced torture or execution. But with clever teamwork, Pilecki and his group found ways.

Sometimes, a prisoner working in the camp's workshops or kitchens might trade small favors with local Polish workers who were forced to do jobs near the camp. On rare occasions, these locals could carry notes hidden in their clothes or inside crates of supplies. Other times, a released prisoner—someone who had completed a forced labor sentence—was secretly given coded messages to take back to the Resistance in Warsaw. It was unbelievably risky. Many would have refused. But Pilecki's group believed that the truth had to escape, no matter the cost.

Bit by bit, word began to reach the Polish Resistance. They learned about the inhumane conditions, the disappearances, and the extreme cruelty. But many outsiders still found it hard to accept the staggering scale of the Nazis' actions. Some people abroad thought the reports must be exaggerated. Pilecki wrote in his secret diary, "We had hoped the world would react at once, but we found that our voices struggled to be believed."

Inside the camp, disease spread quickly, and the work was exhausting. Pilecki often saw friends and fellow prisoners become too weak to continue. Yet he encouraged everyone who could still stand to remain hopeful, to believe there was a purpose in their suffering. "If we can hold on and pass our message," he told them, "maybe we can save countless others." But as months turned into years, Pilecki realized something else. He couldn't keep smuggling out these reports forever. There might come a time when he had to escape if he wanted to present everything in person to the Polish Resistance leadership. Escaping from Auschwitz seemed impossible—there were high-voltage fences, armed watchtowers, and rows of guards with attack dogs. Most who tried were caught quickly. Even if someone slipped out of the camp, they had to cross many miles of hostile territory to reach safety.

DARING FOR FREEDOM

In April 1943, after nearly three years in Auschwitz, Pilecki and two fellow prisoners decided it was time to take their biggest risk yet. One night, they made a bold move. They cut power to a bakery outside the main camp where they worked, slipped past a guard, and rushed into the darkness. Guards noticed they were missing and started a frantic search. Shots rang out, and dogs barked in the distance, but Pilecki and his companions pressed on, moving swiftly through fields and forests. Every moment, they feared being spotted by Nazi patrols or betrayed by frightened villagers. Somehow, luck and determination guided them. After days of hiding and traveling at night, they reached a safe house belonging to the Polish underground movement. A fellow resistance fighter later recalled Pilecki's arrival: "He came in, exhausted and hungry, but his spirit was as strong as ever. He carried pages of notes—proof of what was truly happening in Auschwitz."

Once free, Pilecki wrote a detailed report about the horrors he had witnessed—everything from forced labor, starvation, and disease, to even the most horrible of crimes. He described daily life in the camp so that no one could claim ignorance. He named high-ranking Nazi officers and even listed the numbers assigned to certain prisoners who had disappeared. It was the first comprehensive eyewitness account of what was happening inside Auschwitz.

Members of the Polish Resistance quickly sent his report to the Polish government-in-exile (the official Polish government that had relocated to London) and to Allied nations like Britain and the United States. They hoped that once people learned the truth, they would take immediate action—perhaps bomb the railroad tracks leading into Auschwitz, or at least confirm that such cruelty was taking place. Unfortunately, the reaction was not as strong as they had hoped. Many government officials outside Poland found the stories too terrible to believe or claimed there were other military priorities. Still, Pilecki's courage meant that the truth was now on record. There was no longer any excuse for the world to say, "We didn't know."

Even after escaping from Auschwitz, Pilecki did not stop fighting. He took part in the Warsaw Uprising of 1944, when Polish resistance fighters rose up against the occupying German forces in a last-ditch effort to free their capital. Although the uprising was eventually crushed, Pilecki's determination never waned. He continued to risk his life for Poland's freedom. People who met Pilecki described him as quiet, humble, and deeply caring. He rarely boasted about what he had done in Auschwitz, yet his very presence inspired others. "Witold's calmness under pressure was remarkable," a Warsaw Uprising comrade recalled. "He had already endured the worst imaginable. There was nothing left that could break his spirit."

When World War II ended in 1945, the full extent of Nazi crimes in Auschwitz and other camps finally became widely known. Countries around the globe were shocked by the evidence of what Pilecki and other survivors had been reporting for years. Photographs, documents, and the testimonies of thousands of liberated prisoners confirmed the unimaginable horror. These revelations were a key factor in bringing Nazi leaders to justice. Many were put on trial for war crimes, and the world recognized that such atrocities must never happen again. Pilecki's reports—started in the depths of Auschwitz—played a major part in shaping global awareness of the Holocaust. Historians now say his bravery forced the issue into the spotlight earlier than it might have reached on its own. If the world had believed him sooner, more lives might have been saved, but his testimony still proved invaluable in holding the Nazis accountable.

THE PILECKI LEGACY

For many years, Pilecki's name was not widely known outside Poland. But in recent decades, more and more people have discovered his story, amazed that someone would volunteer to enter the notorious Auschwitz camp. He has been called one of the greatest heroes of World War II.

What makes Witold Pilecki's story so important for us today? It shows that one person's courage and determination can bring vital truths to light, even in the darkest of times. Pilecki risked his life, not for glory or fame, but because he believed that knowing the truth is the first step toward changing the world. He realized that if no one reported what was happening, the Nazis could continue their cruelty in secret. Even though it took time for the world to believe him, his reports and personal testimony laid the groundwork for future investigations. His bravery helped shorten the war's illusions and contributed to the Nazis' eventual defeat, because an enemy that operates in total secrecy has more power than one whose crimes are exposed.

In the years since, historians, authors, and even film producers have shared Pilecki's story around the globe. Children in Poland learn about him in school, and grown-ups in many countries have come to see him as a symbol of moral courage. That's because he showed the power of love, loyalty, and unbreakable resolve. If you ever feel that you're just one person who can't possibly make a difference, remember Pilecki's courage, which knew no limits. "His mission into Auschwitz remains one of the boldest acts of defiance in recorded history," is how one historian recently put it.

Pilecki walked straight into one of the worst places imaginable, determined to reveal the truth to the world. He never lost hope, and he never lost faith that doing what's right could help change the world's future.

The Night Witches

Somewhere on the Eastern Front of World War II, tiny biplanes soared low over the countryside in the middle of the night. Their engines barely hummed as they glided close to enemy lines. The German soldiers below could not see them, only hear a faint *whoosh*—like a breeze brushing against the trees. These mysterious, silent attackers were the Night Witches, a group of brave Soviet women who flew nighttime bombing missions in flimsy, old-fashioned aircraft. Despite being underestimated by many, they became legends for their daring and skill.

The Night Witches were officially known as the 588th Night Bomber Regiment of the Soviet Air Force. They were formed in 1941 by a famous female pilot named Marina Raskova, who was determined to prove that women could fight in the air just as courageously as men. The Soviet Union needed all the help it could get after Germany invaded. Although some leaders doubted women had the strength or courage for combat, Raskova convinced them otherwise, and three all-female regiments were created. The 588th quickly gained the most attention and, eventually, the nickname "Night Witches." One pilot, Nadezhda Popova, later wrote in her diary, "We were young, and we were eager to defend our country. Night after night, we soared into the darkness, hoping our courage would shine where light could not." From the moment they signed up, these women faced challenges right away: the shortage of supplies, the rough conditions of life on the front, and, probably, the biggest obstacle of them all, The doubts of their male counterparts.

HANDICAPPED FROM THE START

The Night Witches flew Polikarpov Po-2 biplanes, which were originally designed for training and crop-dusting. Made primarily of wood and fabric, they had open cockpits—meaning there was no roof protecting the pilots and navigators from the freezing winds of high altitude. They were also painfully slow, topping out at around 90 miles per hour. Some people called them "flying sewing machines" because of the engine's rattling sounds.

At first, these flimsy planes seemed like a major disadvantage. However, the biplanes were surprisingly good at nighttime stealth. They couldn't carry heavy bombs, but their lightweight design let them approach enemy lines in near silence. "Our planes were simple, but that was our greatest weapon," One Night Witch said, "No one expected us. And by the time they heard our engines, it was already too late."

The pilots developed a clever trick to increase their element of surprise: They cut the engine just before reaching their target, gliding silently to drop their bombs. This technique gave the Germans little time to react, causing panic among the soldiers below.

The Germans, who were on the receiving end of these silent attacks, began calling the pilots *Nachthexen*, which means "Night Witches" in German. Why witches? Because the slow, fluttering noise of the biplanes as they swooped in reminded them of broomsticks sweeping through the sky. It was spooky, especially in the dead of night. But the women took pride in the nickname. They believed it reflected their power and courage, and they made it a symbol of their unit. One pilot joked, "If they think we're witches, then let's be the best kind of witches—unstoppable ones!"

The Night Witches worked in pairs: one pilot and one navigator. They often flew multiple bombing runs every single night. After dropping bombs on a target, they would circle back, land at a makeshift airfield, quickly reload, and take off again. Some nights, they flew as many as eight missions before dawn! They had to cope with freezing temperatures. Bundled in warm coats and scarves, they still faced biting winds in the open cockpit. The engine's roar pounded in their ears, and the darkness made it hard to see. Tracing their route on a small map under dim light, navigators guided pilots over rivers and fields, making sure they reached their targets undetected. When they weren't flying, these women slept in cramped tents or bunkers, often exhausted from repeated missions. There was also the danger that the enemy could bomb their airfields at any moment. Yet they supported one another with a spirit of camaraderie. The sisterhood they formed was like no other.

Despite the tricky conditions, the Night Witches accomplished astonishing feats. They flew close to the ground to avoid detection by radar, sometimes just tree-top high. German searchlights would scan the sky, anti-aircraft guns would fire blindly, and yet those brave aviators pressed on. If hit, their planes offered almost no protection, but bailing out was also a gamble as they often didn't even have parachutes. Nadezhda Popova recalled one intense night: "We had already flown twice that night, and we were heading out for a third mission. Suddenly, searchlights lit up the sky like a thousand suns, and we heard bullets whizzing past. My navigator and I held our breath, hoping our tiny plane would slip away. We managed to escape unharmed. We laughed later, but at the time, our hearts pounded like never before!" Such moments tested their nerves constantly. Yet each successful mission inspired the next one. They refused to be grounded by fear.

EARNING THEIR WINGS

Over time, even those who doubted the Night Witches came to recognize their skill and bravery. Some male pilots admitted that these women were among the most dedicated fliers in the entire Soviet Air Force. The Night Witches completed more than 23,000 missions overall—an incredible number that is a testament to their determination. "I wouldn't have believed it if I hadn't seen it," a male Soviet officer once said, "Night after night, these young women climb into those old planes, vanish into darkness, and return with stories of successful raids. They have earned the highest respect on this front. Many of the Night Witches received prestigious awards and medals for their heroism. Some even became aces, recognized for numerous successful missions. Yet despite all the honors, they often remained modest, saying they were just doing their part to defend their homeland. So, how did these daring nighttime raids change the course of the war? First, they disrupted German supply lines and frontline positions, making it more difficult for the enemy to hold conquered territories. Every bomb drop, every surprise raid meant fewer resources for the Nazi army. Second, they boosted Soviet morale at a time when hope was in short supply. People who heard about the Night Witches felt a surge of pride: if these young women could stand up to the Nazis in such a fearless way, perhaps victory was possible after all.

Their impact also went beyond military outcomes. The Night Witches inspired women everywhere to break barriers and prove their worth in roles traditionally reserved for men. By taking flight in outdated biplanes, they soared to new heights of courage and redefined what was possible. They showed that skill, determination, and a little creativity could overcome challenges—no matter how big or small.

When the war ended in 1945, the Night Witches had become an almost mythical force. They proved that bravery has no gender and that even the most unlikely pilots could become legends. Many historians consider them one of the most remarkable air units of all time—particularly because they achieved so much with so little. Their story lived on in memoirs, interviews, and photographs of their ragtag planes and smiling faces. Although time has passed, their legacy reminds us that ordinary people can do extraordinary things when they refuse to give up. Their nightly battles in the dark were a testament to how far determination and unity can carry us—even when the odds are steep.

AN INCREDIBLE FORCE

The Night Witches changed more than just the course of the war; they changed how we think about who can be a hero. With every mission, they challenged old ideas about women's roles in the military. They showed that in the darkest times, courage can light the way to victory.

Today, we can look to the Night Witches and see examples of teamwork, resourcefulness, and fearlessness. They remind us that no matter how small or simple our tools may seem—like their wooden biplanes—we can still make a big difference if we refuse to quit. Their story encourages us to face life's challenges head-on, with eyes on the horizon and hearts full of hope.

As you turn the pages to learn about other inspiring stories of World War II, remember the Night Witches' lessons: remain daring in the face of danger, lean on your friends when times are tough, and never forget that even the quietest whisper can roar like thunder when supported by boldness.

The Tuskegee Airmen

As World War II raged on, stories of courage and determination were springing up across the whole world. One of the most inspiring came from a group of African American pilots known as the Tuskegee Airmen. These men not only fought bravely against the Axis powers, but they also battled racism and prejudice at home. Through their grit, skill, and unwavering spirit, they broke barriers and proved that heroes can come from anywhere—no matter the color of their skin.

As we saw from Dorie Miller's chapter, Before World War II, many people in the United States believed that African Americans did not have what it took to fight in the armed forces. When it came specifically to the Air Force, some people thought black people lacked the bravery or intelligence required to fly advanced warplanes. It was a harmful myth, but one shared by too many in power. When the war began, the U.S. government needed more pilots—and public pressure finally convinced leaders to open a special flight training program for African Americans — a program took place at Tuskegee Army Air Field, located in Tuskegee, Alabama. "They told us we couldn't fly. I showed up to prove that we could," said one of the first cadets to enroll.

Training at Tuskegee was no walk in the park. It included countless hours of classroom study, where cadets learned about aircraft mechanics, navigation, and meteorology. Then came hands-on instruction in small planes, followed by advanced tactics in fighter aircraft. In addition to the tough academic and physical requirements, these cadets faced racism from some officers who didn't believe in their abilities. Yet, the future Tuskegee Airmen refused to give up. They pushed themselves to become excellent pilots, determined to show that skill, discipline, and dedication mattered far more than skin color. "We studied late into the night. Our eyes burned from reading manuals, but we knew every page would help us become the pilots we dreamed of being," said one cadet.

Upon graduation, the newly minted pilots were assigned to segregated units, meaning they served separately from white airmen. Their most famous group was the 332nd Fighter Group, which became known for flying aircraft with bright red tail markings. Because of those colorful tails, they were often called the "Red Tails." As the war raged on, bomber crews flying deep into enemy territory needed protection from enemy fighter planes. This was a dangerous job—German pilots would do everything they could to shoot down Allied bombers. The Tuskegee Airmen took to the skies as escorts, defending these bombers with skill and bravery. Their orders were clear: keep the bombers safe at all costs. And that's exactly what they did.

CHALLENGES ON ALL SIDES

As the war progressed, Bomber crews began to notice that when Tuskegee Airmen were on guard, and they realised comrades made it home more often when guarded by the Red Tails. Stories spread of how the Tuskegee Airmen never abandoned their bombers, sticking to them like protectors no matter how heavy the enemy fire became. Soon, even the initial doubters had to admit these pilots were not just good—they were among the best. One bomber pilot, grateful for the Tuskegee Airmen's escort, later said, "We felt safer when we saw those red-tailed fighters above us. They stayed with us the whole mission. We knew they had our backs." Neverthelss, when these heroes returned to base, they often faced segregation. They might have fought side by side with white pilots during the battle, but on the ground, they weren't allowed in the same clubs or housing. Such unfairness fueled their determination to keep proving their worth.

By the end of the war, the Tuskegee Airmen had flown a total of 311 missions during World War II, 179 of which were bomber escort missions in Europe and North Africa. Their efforts made a real difference in slowing down enemy forces and protecting Allied aircraft. The Nazi fighters realized that challenging the Red Tails was no easy fight—these skilled pilots knew exactly how to outmaneuver them. By protecting Allied bombers so effectively, the Tuskegee Airmen helped weaken the Axis powers. Each mission deprived Nazi Germany of vital war equipment, forcing them to spread out their defenses. Allied forces gained a significant advantage in the skies over Europe, hastening the day when the war would finally end.

Because of their outstanding record, the Tuskegee Airmen earned respect from the highest levels of the U.S. military. Many received awards such as the Distinguished Flying Cross for acts of heroism. Some Tuskegee pilots became flying aces, taking down multiple enemy planes in air-to-air combat. Yet, their greatest achievement was showing the world that African American pilots were just as capable as any other.

Colonel Benjamin O. Davis Jr., one of the most famous Tuskegee Airmen and their commander, summed it up nicely by saying, "We didn't want any handouts. We just wanted a chance to prove we could do the job." Such words came to define the Tuskegee spirit. Their courage went beyond the battlefield, extending into the realm of social change. They brought hope to many Americans who had felt overlooked and discriminated against. When news spread of these African American pilots safeguarding entire squadrons of bombers, it inspired countless people to believe in a future where racial barriers could be torn down. Their story became a shining example that skill and courage know no color—only dedication and heart.

LEGACY

In 1948, President Harry Truman signed an executive order that officially ended segregation in the Armed Forces. This change did not happen overnight, but the successes of the Tuskegee Airmen played a major role in convincing leaders and citizens alike that discrimination was both unfair and harmful to military strength.

Many Tuskegee veterans continued serving in the newly integrated military, rising to higher ranks and becoming trailblazers for future generations. Some worked as mentors, engineers, or instructors, sharing their knowledge and encouraging others to pursue their dreams, no matter the obstacles. Their influence reached far beyond flight lines and airfields, inspiring an entire nation to strive for equality.

The story of the Tuskegee Airmen reminds us that true heroism involves fighting for more than just yourself. They had to be twice as good just to be viewed as equals. And they rose to the challenge, becoming symbols of courage for everyone who dreams of breaking barriers. The next time you see a plane overhead, think of the Red Tails and how they blazed a trail, proving that greatness can come from anyone, anywhere, as long as they never give up on their dreams.

Schindler's Jews

One of the most important figures to emerge from WWII was a tall, confident gentleman who liked to dress in fine suits. To the naked eye, he was more a businessman than a hero. Still, this man ended up emerging as one of the most enigmatic names of World War 2, with his kindness saving the lives of more than a thousand people during one of the darkest chapters in human history.

Oskar Schindler was born in 1908 in what is now the Czech Republic. He grew up in a reasonably comfortable home, learning early on the importance of making deals and turning a profit. When Germany invaded Poland in 1939, he saw an opportunity to make money by running factories that produced enamelware—pots, pans, and other metal items needed for the war effort. He enjoyed a luxurious lifestyle, mingling with high-ranking Nazi officers and throwing lavish parties. Yet, beneath this polished appearance, Schindler noticed the cruel way Jewish people were being treated under Nazi rule. Jews were forced out of their homes, robbed of their belongings, and sent to harsh ghettos or labor camps. At first, Schindler kept his focus on business. But something in him began to change as he witnessed the growing terror around him.

In 1939, Schindler took over an old factory in Kraków, Poland, renaming it Deutsche Emailwarenfabrik, often called "Emalia." He needed workers, and he knew that the German authorities were placing Jewish men and women in forced labor. If they had jobs in factories deemed essential for the war, they had a slightly better chance of avoiding deportation to concentration camps. So, Schindler hired as many Jews as he could, telling Nazi officials that this labor was necessary for his production lines. One Jewish worker named Moshe Bejski later remembered his first impression of Schindler: "He seemed like a businessman, but when he looked at you, he had a kindness in his eyes. I could not understand why a man like him would care at all about us."

Although Schindler's original goal may have been to keep his factory running, he soon realized these jobs could actually save lives. Whenever a Nazi officer questioned his workforce, Schindler used his charm and connections to protect them. He hosted gatherings for the Nazi elite, ensuring he stayed on their good side. In this way, Schindler created a safe haven within the walls of his factory—even if it wasn't entirely clear to everyone why he was doing it.

A GROWING COMPASSION

As months passed, conditions for Jews in Kraków got worse. The Nazis forced them into a cramped ghetto, brutally clearing out entire neighborhoods. Families were split apart, possessions were confiscated, and fear became constant. Schindler's workers would arrive at the factory exhausted and terrified, unsure if their loved ones were still alive. Their stories began to affect Schindler more deeply than he ever expected. He started making changes to help them. He would allow workers to sleep in the factory if they had no safe place to return to. He created a clinic to treat minor injuries and illnesses. He also bribed Nazi officers to leave his workers alone. One of his Jewish employees, Helen Jonas, later stated, "He took enormous risks so that we could feel a small shred of dignity. It was the first time in a long while that we felt someone actually cared." It was becoming clear that Schindler was no longer just a businessman. He was evolving into a protector, someone who recognized a grave injustice and decided to stand against it—even if it meant endangering himself.

In 1943, the Nazi regime decided to clear out the Kraków Ghetto entirely, sending many of the remaining Jews to the Plaszów concentration camp. Suddenly, Schindler's workers were in immediate danger. Plaszów was run by a cruel commander named Amon Göth, a man notorious for his brutal treatment of prisoners. Schindler realized that if his employees were transferred to Plaszów, their chances of survival were slim.

Risking his own safety, Schindler convinced Göth that his factory was crucial to the German war machine. He persuaded him to let his workers stay in the factory compound instead of living in the main camp. This was an enormous favor to ask. Still, Schindler used his connections, money, and charm, explaining that his production line could not be disturbed if they expected good results. Göth, interested in gaining bribes and maintaining a reputation with important Nazi officials, agreed.

A SECOND CHANCE AT LIFE

It was a huge triumph for Schindler and his workers, but the danger didn't end. Every week, new orders arrived to send more Jews to forced labor or death camps. Yet, Schindler fought on, using every trick he knew to keep "his Jews," as he called them, safe. Sometimes, he even claimed elderly or sick workers were essential mechanics so they wouldn't be taken away.

By 1944, the war had turned against Germany. The Nazis, losing on several fronts, started closing some camps and forcing prisoners on death marches or shipping them to even more lethal places like Auschwitz. Schindler realized that Plaszów would likely be shut down, and his workers could be at risk of being sent to extermination camps. He hatched a plan: move his entire factory to the region of Moravia (in what is now the Czech Republic), well away from the front lines. If he could relocate, he might rescue his workers from inevitable doom.

This was a massive undertaking. Schindler spent a fortune on bribes, paperwork, and transport, insisting that the hundreds of Jews who worked for him were necessary to continue his "vital war production." In reality, he was building a safe haven. The final test was to create a list of the workers he needed—this became famously known as "Schindler's List." Each name on that list represented a life that could be saved. A survivor later said, "Seeing my name on Schindler's list was like having a second chance at life. We prayed for the day when the war would end, and we could leave that nightmare behind."

After weeks of tense negotiations, Schindler managed to relocate more than a thousand of his workers to a new factory in Brünnlitz (Brno-Líšeň area). Though still under Nazi control, it was far safer than the brutal concentration camps. He continued to operate his factory, but only on paper. The truth was he rarely produced much for the war effort, and he quietly sabotaged any manufacturing that might actually help the Nazi cause. All the while, he made sure his workers had enough food, clothing, and protection. Smuggling supplies into the factory was risky, but Schindler did it anyway. He wanted to ensure no one starved or froze. When inspectors visited, he used his silver tongue to convince them everything was under control. Sometimes, he would distract them with fine meals and gifts so they wouldn't inspect too closely.

"If this factory can stand until the war ends, then we live," one worker wrote in a hidden journal. "It's our last shield against oblivion." Schindler knew it too, and it weighed on him every hour of every day.

As 1945 approached, the collapse of Nazi Germany became more likely. Allied forces advanced on all fronts, and the horrors of the Holocaust were beginning to come to light. Schindler's factory in Brünnlitz was still running, sheltering Jewish workers who might otherwise have perished.

Finally, in May 1945, the war in Europe ended. Nazi Germany surrendered. Freedom arrived at last for the hundreds of people on Schindler's list.

Many couldn't believe they were still alive to see it. The day after the factory shut its doors, Soviet troops arrived, and the survivors rejoiced. They had lived through a nightmare, and it was largely thanks to one man's determination. Schindler, however, knew Soviet authorities could target him for his earlier connections to the Nazi Party. He left his factory and fled westward with his wife, Emilie. They took a letter signed by the Jewish workers, describing how Schindler had saved their lives. It would become his only shield if anyone accused him of war crimes because of his Nazi membership.

SAVING LIVES TRUMPED MAKING MONEY

After the war, Schindler struggled to succeed in business again, moving from one venture to another. He never regained the wealth he once had. But for the people he saved—often called "Schindlerjuden" (Schindler's Jews)—he was a hero. They looked after him in later years, raising money so he could visit Israel, where many of them had settled. In 1963, the Israeli government honored Oskar Schindler by naming him Righteous Among the Nations, a unique title given to non-Jews who risked their lives to save Jews during the Holocaust. Former worker Leopold Page recalled, "Without Schindler, I wouldn't be here today. He owed us nothing, but he gave us our lives back."

Schindler died in 1974, largely unknown outside the community of survivors he had protected. Over time, though, the world would learn his story in more detail, thanks to books and, later, a famous Steven Spielberg movie that brought attention to his efforts.

His actions also served as a powerful reminder that not everyone in Nazi Germany was evil or blindly followed orders. Schindler started off as someone who wanted to make money, yet ended up risking everything—his fortune, his safety, and his future—for the sake of others. In doing so, he gave the world a lasting message: even in the darkest times, compassion and courage can shine through.

One of the most famous lines often associated with Schindler's rescue efforts is a quote from the Talmud (a Jewish religious text): "Whoever saves one life saves the world entire." Schindler saved more than a thousand, and each of those people carried forward the spark of hope he provided.

Oskar Schindler's journey teaches us that courage can take many forms. It doesn't always roar with the sound of cannons; sometimes, it whispers through acts of quiet rescue. By protecting over a thousand Jews from almost certain death, he ensured that thousands of survivors and their descendants could live peacefully around the globe for many years to come.

And so, while Schindler didn't change the outcome of World War II on a grand scale, he changed the outcome for the men, women, and children he protected. In doing so, he became one of the war's most inspirational figures. His story—filled with drama, danger, and redemption—continues to guide us toward kindness and empathy in our own lives. After all, as the survivors of Schindler's List can tell you, little actions you take could mean *everything* to someone else.

The Nisei Unit

It's the middle of the war, and as nations clash across continents, and the skies rumble with fighter planes, a unique crop of American soldiers begin to rise to fame. They are the 442nd Regimental Combat Team, formed mostly by second-generation Japanese Americans, or "Nisei," and they are gaining prominence due to their incredible bravery in tough circumstances.

TOUGH START

As we saw in Chapter 1, When Japan attacked Pearl Harbor on December 7, 1941, the United States entered the war. For Japanese Americans already living in the U.S., life turned upside down. Many Americans questioned their loyalty, and unjust treatment followed. Over 100,000 Japanese Americans were forced into "internment camps," losing their homes, businesses, and freedom. An internment camp was essentially a secure facility where Japanese Americans were forcibly relocated and confined during World War II. Young American men suddenly found themselves labeled "enemy aliens" in their own country.

Despite this unfairness, many Nisei still longed to prove their loyalty to the United States—the only country they had ever called home. They wanted a chance to fight against the Axis powers (Germany, Italy, and Japan) and show that they were just as patriotic as any other Americans. Eventually, the U.S. government agreed to form an all-Japanese American combat team. It was officially called the 442nd Regimental Combat Team, and it included both volunteers and men drafted from the internment camps. Their motto was "Go for Broke," meaning they would give it everything they had, no matter the cost.

In early 1943, Japanese American recruits began arriving at Camp

Shelby, Mississippi, to start their training. For many, it was a shocking change. Some had grown up in cities like Los Angeles or Seattle, while others had come from internment camps in remote parts of the country. Mississippi's hot, humid climate and tough training routines tested their resolve. They learned to march in formation, crawl under barbed wire, and fire rifles with accuracy. In spare moments, they sang songs or told jokes, they had to make the best out of a bad situation. "I missed my family, and I felt angry that they were in a camp. But I believed if I could serve well, I might help them and show the world what we were worth,"one Nisei soldier, Masao Ogoro, said.

Their instructors were impressed by the recruits' determination. These young men woke up early each morning and practiced late into the night, after all, they felt like they had something to prove: that their hearts beat as true for America as anyone else's. By the time they finished training, the 442nd was ready to be deployed to Europe, where some of the fiercest fighting raged on.

In 1944, the 442nd sailed across the Atlantic, heading first to Italy. The mountainous terrain and enemy strongholds made every battle a challenge. Italian hills were lined with German soldiers determined to stop the Allies from advancing north. Rain turned dirt into mud, and steep slopes offered little cover. Yet the 442nd pressed on, climbing rocky heights and pushing through enemy lines.

Soon after Italy, they fought in France. The Allies needed help driving the Germans back, and the 442nd was called in for the job. The men trudged through thick forests and faced ambushes, mortar fire, and snipers. But their courage never wavered. One German officer, once captured, reportedly expressed surprise that these "small Japanese American soldiers" fought with such fierce spirit. He confessed that he and his men had underestimated them, to their own cost.

THE RESCUE OF THE "LOST BATTALION"

One of the most famous battles involving the 442nd took place in the Vosges Mountains of eastern France. In October 1944, a group of Texas soldiers, known as the "Lost Battalion," became trapped behind German lines. Surrounded by enemy troops, they were running low on supplies and had no easy way out. The 442nd was called in to rescue them.

For days, the Japanese American unit battled through thick fog, tall trees, and relentless German gunfire. Casualties mounted; many of their own were wounded or killed. Yet they refused to turn back, determined to reach the trapped Texans. A 442nd soldier, poignantly touching on their own experience back home, said "We knew what it was like to be abandoned, so we weren't going to abandon them. We kept going—inch by inch—until we got them out."

Finally, after continuous assaults, they broke through the enemy's defense. The 442nd saved about 200 Texan soldiers, and although they lost many of their own in the process, it proved to be a great success story for the allies. Survivors from the Lost Battalion were stunned by the dedication and bravery of the Japanese American troops who fought so tirelessly to free them. After the rescue, word spread throughout the Allied armies. The 442nd had achieved the impossible in the Vosges Mountains, and people across the U.S. began to realize the sacrifice and heroism of these Japanese American soldiers. Their actions made headlines: stories of fearless charges, incredible rescues, and unwavering determination.

Back home, families still sat behind barbed wire in internment camps, hearing about the heroic deeds of their sons and brothers. It was a bittersweet victory. Even as the 442nd gained a reputation as one of the most formidable combat units in the war, their loved ones were not yet free from discrimination. Nonetheless, the men pressed on, believing that every success on the battlefield would shine a light on the unfair treatment endured by Japanese Americans.

A few soldiers kept diaries or wrote letters whenever they could. Daniel Inouye, a future U.S. Senator, served with the 442nd and lost his right arm in battle. He later said, "I believed that being an American was more than a matter of where my parents came from. It was a matter of conviction—a belief in the principles of freedom and justice." Another soldier, Susumu Ito, wrote home:

"When it's dark out here, with artillery lighting the sky, I imagine I'm back home in California, free to walk wherever I like. I dream that maybe, if we win, we can all walk free again one day."

These words captured the mixture of hope, fear, and determination felt by the 442nd. Each soldier carried the weight of two battles: one against the Axis powers and one against prejudice back home.

OVERDUE PRAISE

By the war's end in 1945, the 442nd had become known as the most highly decorated unit for its size and length of service in the entire history of the U.S. military. They earned thousands of awards, including the prestigious Distinguished Service Cross and the Medal of Honor. However, for many years, not all these awards were immediately recognized. It wasn't until decades later that some soldiers from the 442nd finally received the honors they truly deserved. Looking back, historians have noted that perhaps the reason why the 442nd fought with such bravery was because they wanted to prove they belonged—that they were just as American as anyone else risking their life for freedom. They fought not only for victory overseas but for the future acceptance of Japanese Americans in the country they loved. "We fought for a country that didn't always believe in us. But that made us fight harder, because we believed in our country," one Nisei veteran said.

When the survivors of the 442nd returned to the United States, they came back as heroes in the eyes of many of their fellow soldiers. But they still faced challenges. Some found that their families were still in internment camps or had lost their homes and businesses. Others struggled to find jobs because of lingering prejudice. It was a harsh reminder that, even after risking their lives for their country, they had to continue fighting for dignity and respect.

Yet, changes were happening. The stories of the 442nd's daring rescues and relentless courage had spread far and wide. People who once doubted Japanese Americans began to question their own assumptions. Over time, laws that discriminated against Asians in America were challenged and overturned. The bravery of the 442nd had helped open the door to new attitudes, forging a path toward greater fairness and equality.

Today, the 442nd's legacy lives on as an example of courage and unity. In 2010, the U.S. Congress awarded members of the 442nd (and related units) the Congressional Gold Medal, one of the highest civilian honors. This recognition came long after the war ended, but it showed that the nation finally acknowledged their extraordinary service. By that time, many veterans were elderly or had passed away, but their families and descendants accepted the honor in their name.

The story of the 442nd Regimental Combat Team resonates because it's about people who believed in themselves and their country, even when that country did not fully believe in them. They found a way to transform pain and distrust into acts of heroism on the battlefield. Their role in significant battles helped the Allies push forward, making a real difference in the fight against fascism. More importantly, their story influenced how Americans view liberty, justice, and equality. The men of 442nd showed that with determination, unity, and a strong belief in yourself, *anyone* can "go for broke" and make history—just like they did.

Mad Jack Churchill

Of all the characters in WWII, no one was as unique or as fearlessly eccentric as Jack "Mad Jack" Churchill. By the time World War 2 broke, modern warfare had changed drastically to what it had been 100 years prior, so when a British soldier charged into battles wielding a longbow, a sword, and playing the bagpipes—yes, bagpipes! — he was always going to go down in history!

Jack Churchill was born in 1906 in Hong Kong, which was then a British colony. He moved around with his family as a boy, eventually returning to England. He had an early love for music, particularly bagpipes, even though Scotland was not his home region. He also discovered a passion for archery, practicing tirelessly until his skill with a longbow was second to none. When he wasn't shooting arrows into targets, he could often be found honing his swordsmanship or learning new tunes on the pipes.

His family and friends found Jack charming but unusual. One schoolmate remembered, "He always seemed to look for excitement where the rest of us saw none. If there was a challenge, he wanted in. If there was a quiet moment, he'd stir it up somehow."

After completing his education, Jack joined the British Army. Yet even there, he stood out. He carried his bow and sword on training exercises, insisting they kept him "mentally sharp." Some officers chuckled at his old-fashioned ways, but no one doubted his dedication. When World War II broke out in 1939, Jack Churchill sprang into action. At a time when tanks, airplanes, and automatic guns ruled the battlefield, the idea of using a longbow and a sword seemed absurd. But Jack never let that stop him. He had a motto: "Any officer who goes into action without his sword is improperly dressed." He took these words seriously. In fact, he became famous for leading men into combat with his Claymore sword—a large Scottish blade that demanded both strength and courage to wield effectively. Jack's fellow soldiers were inspired and amazed by his determination to keep older battle traditions alive. As one comrade recalled, "He made you believe that bravery wasn't about having the biggest gun. It was about having the biggest heart."

FIRST GLIMPSES OF "MAD JACK"

Jack's early wartime exploits occurred in France in 1940, when the German Army's lightning-fast tactics forced the British into a chaotic retreat. Amidst the confusion, Jack stood out. Legend says he achieved the last confirmed longbow kill in military history during this period, launching an arrow into an unsuspecting German soldier from the shadows. It sounded like something from a medieval story, but witnesses swore it really happened. Soon, people began calling him "Mad Jack" because he did things no one else would even dream of. He fearlessly biked across enemy lines to gather intelligence. He led small raiding parties armed with nothing more than his trusted sword. One moment, you'd hear bagpipes in the distance; the next, you'd see Jack charging forward with unstoppable enthusiasm. Even while the British were being pushed back to the beaches of Dunkirk, Jack continued to fight. After returning to England, he refused to rest. He volunteered for a new unit: the Commandos—elite fighters trained for daring operations in enemy territory. It was the perfect place for a man who thrived on danger and surprise attacks.

One of Mad Jack's most famous moments happened in December 1941 during a raid on the Norwegian island of Vågsoy. Jack insisted on spearheading the assault. As the landing craft approached the shore, he stood at the front, playing bagpipes under enemy fire (he played "March of the Cameron Men" for those of you asking.) Once they landed, he flung the pipes aside, raised his sword, and sprinted forward. His men, inspired by their fearless leader, followed without hesitation. It is said that captured German soldiers would often think that Jack was a trick from the army - a diversion; after all, who would attack with bagpipes?! It wasn't a trick, however; it was simply Jack Churchill's way of announcing his arrival. He believed music could rally his own troops and rattle the enemy. Though bullets tore through the chilly air, the Commandos overwhelmed the German defenders and secured vital positions. Jack personally captured several enemy soldiers at sword point. The entire raid was a success, damaging German operations and boosting the morale of Allied forces. Jack's flamboyant tactics further cemented his reputation as a fearless warrior who could turn the tide of battle.

Mad Jack's bravery often paid off but also led him into incredibly risky situations. In 1943, Churchill and his Commandos fought in Italy, pushing the Germans north. During one night mission, Jack found himself cut off from the rest of his unit. Undeterred, he kept fighting until he was surrounded. He tried to hold off the enemy, playing a slow lament on his pipes in defiance. Eventually, German soldiers overwhelmed him, and Mad Jack was taken prisoner. Even in captivity, he refused to let fear consume him. German guards must have been amazed to see a captive who wore a kilt, played bagpipes, and approached them with cheerful conversation. Jack was moved to several prisoner-of-war camps, including the infamous Sachsenhausen concentration camp in Germany.

In typical Mad Jack fashion, captivity didn't hold him for long. He staged a daring escape from Sachsenhausen, crawling under a barbed-wire fence in the dead of night. The plan required stealth, courage, and luck—qualities he seemed to have in abundance. Although he was recaptured a short time later, he showed no remorse. He simply waited for the next opportunity.

Later, he was transferred to a different camp in Austria. Once again, he plotted an escape. This time, he slipped past guards and began walking east, hoping to reach Allied lines. For days, he trudged through forests and mountains, dodging enemy patrols. In the end, he stumbled upon an American armored unit that could barely believe the ragged figure who claimed to be a British Commando. They quickly verified his identity and welcomed him back to freedom.

By the time Jack returned from captivity, the war in Europe was nearly over. Despite that, he was eager to keep fighting—this time in the Far East, against Imperial Japan. He traveled to Burma (now Myanmar), where a brutal conflict raged. To his disappointment, the war ended before he could see much action there. When he heard the news of Japan's surrender in August 1945, Mad Jack is rumored to have said, "If it wasn't for those Yanks, we could have kept the war going another ten years." He wasn't actually advocating for more war; he was just a soldier who thrived in chaos and felt somewhat deflated that the world no longer needed his peculiar brand of heroism.

LIFE AFTER THE WAR

Once World War II ended, Jack Churchill continued to serve in the British Army for a few more years. He spent time as part of the British occupation forces in Palestine, where he reputedly carried out duties with the same mix of discipline and eccentricity. Eventually, he retired to a quieter life, taking up new hobbies and enjoying family life. Yet his exploits couldn't be forgotten. Soldiers who had served with him told stories of the "commando with a sword" or "the piper who wouldn't quit." Over time, newspapers and magazines picked up these stories, further boosting the legend of Mad Jack Churchill. Although some details became exaggerated, many tales were verified by eyewitnesses who insisted that they were absolutely true—yes, he really did charge into battle playing bagpipes, and yes, he really did prefer a sword to a modern firearm.

Many who served alongside Mad Jack had their own memories and quips:

"Churchill did things I'd never seen in any army manual. Yet his men adored him because he led from the front."
Lieutenant Colonel Dudley Shaw

"I doubted my eyes the first time I saw him draw that sword. But the enemy doubted even more. He was a force of nature."
Commando Robert Firth

"He'd joke with us one minute and be launching a daring raid the next. His spirit carried the whole unit."
Soldier John Bennett

Such words clearly showed that Jack Churchill wasn't reckless—he was confident, skilled, and fearless. People couldn't help but rally around him because his determination to press forward seemed unshakeable. In raids on Norway, he boosted morale and achieved surprise victories. In Italy, he proved that even one soldier's courage could disrupt enemy lines. By defying the odds, he inspired those around him to fight harder, push further, and believe in the possibility of success against terrifying odds.

Moreover, his legend served a bigger purpose. Word of his feats spread among Allied troops, convincing them that sheer willpower could conquer fear. For those exhausted by the stress of war, hearing about the officer who led with a sword and bagpipes brought laughter, admiration, and a renewed sense of daring. Jack took pride in standing out from the crowd, not to show off but to spark courage in others. In a time when the entire world seemed to be in darkness, he offered a glimpse of gallantry that felt like it belonged to a different age.

His unwavering spirit is a testament to the idea that determination can be just as powerful as any weapon. He didn't let fear dictate his actions. Instead, he shaped his reality around the belief that anything was possible if he charged forward with confidence—bagpipes singing, arrow notched, and sword shining. Mad Jack exemplified the idea that sometimes, all you need is your heart, your wits, and a little dash of madness to make an unforgettable impact. By marching into battle with a sword when rifles were standard, he showed that heroism often defies expectations—and that confidence in the face of fear can inspire those around you to do the impossible.

America's Most Decorated Soldier

Audie Leon Murphy, a quiet farm boy who stood at just over five feet five inches tall, rose to become probably the most talked about solider in World War 2.

Audie was born in 1925 near Kingston, Texas. His family was poor, and he grew up picking cotton and hunting small game to help feed his siblings. Despite having little schooling, he developed a sharp mind. He also learned to handle a rifle at an early age, quickly becoming a skilled marksman. His father, a day laborer, often wandered away, leaving Audie's mother to raise the children on her own. Tragically, she passed away when Audie was just a teenager. Left without parents, he felt a strong urge to support his younger brothers and sisters. When the United States entered World War II after the attack on Pearl Harbor, Audie saw his chance to earn money and provide for his family. But there was a big obstacle: he was underage. He tried to enlist in the Marines and the paratroopers, but they turned him away because he looked too small and too young. Finally, on his second attempt, the U.S. Army accepted him.

A DETERMINED RECRUIT

In 1942, Audie Murphy arrived at boot camp, where drill instructors initially doubted he would keep up with more robust recruits. However, his persistence soon proved that toughness isn't just about height or weight. A fellow recruit, James Delaney, later said, "Murphy might have been short in stature, but he could march us all into the ground. He refused to quit." His determination impressed many. He excelled in marksmanship tests and adapted quickly to the discipline of military life. He also displayed remarkable calm in stressful drills, hinting at the courage he would later show in real combat. It wasn't long before his officers noticed that this quiet Texan was someone special.

In early 1943, Murphy shipped out to North Africa to join the Allied forces preparing to invade Europe. Not long after, he took part in the invasion of Sicily, learning firsthand the realities of war. The rugged hills, scorching sun, and enemy resistance all tested the newly minted soldier. Yet, Audie pressed forward, his rifle never far from his side. His focus was on the mission, and fellow GIs began to trust him completely. During this campaign, Murphy showed a flash of the bravery for which he would become famous. In one instance, his unit was pinned down by enemy fire. Without waiting for orders, he crawled to a better position, fired with deadly accuracy, and allowed his squad to move safely. A member of that squad, Carl Byrd, recalled: "We thought we were finished. Then Murphy stood up, still barely a man, but he had no fear. He gave us cover so we could advance. I'll never forget that." From Sicily, Murphy and his comrades moved on to mainland Italy, engaging in more hard-fought battles. The conditions were harsh—muddy fields, rugged mountains, and fortified enemy defenses. But every new struggle sharpened Murphy's skills and sense of responsibility.

By mid-1944, the Allies needed fresh forces to land in the south of France in what was called Operation Dragoon. Audie Murphy's division was chosen for this mission. The goal was to push German troops north and join with other Allied units moving east from Normandy. Although overshadowed by the famous D-Day landings, Operation Dragoon was also critical to freeing France from Nazi control. When the landing craft ramp slammed open, Murphy sprinted across the beach, leading his men inland. German forces defended fiercely, but Murphy's leadership kept the American soldiers unified. His unit advanced through hilltop towns and vineyards, clearing out snipers and machine-gun nests. Again, Murphy's actions stood out. He often volunteered for dangerous scouting missions, sneaking behind enemy lines to gather information. His fearless approach boosted morale, with one soldier noting: "If Audie Murphy said we could take a hill, we believed him. He never let fear decide our moves."

By the winter of 1945, as the Allies approached Germany's borders, the fighting intensified. Supplies ran thin, and German resistance became desperate. In late January, near the town of Holtzwihr in eastern France, Murphy's unit faced one of its toughest tests yet. The German army attacked with infantry and tanks, forcing many Americans to retreat to a more defensible position. But Murphy refused to abandon his wounded comrades.

He ordered his men to fall back and prepare a new line of defense, then raced forward alone to an abandoned tank destroyer. Although the vehicle was on fire, its machine gun still worked. Murphy climbed onto it, braving enemy fire. From this exposed spot, he directed artillery strikes over the radio, steering shells onto German tanks. All the while, he fired the machine gun to hold off enemy troops. His ammunition belts fed the weapon as bullets zinged all around him. A stunned observer, Sergeant Elmer Redding, later said: "I've never seen anything like it. He was up there alone, guiding artillery by radio with one hand and firing that machine gun with the other. It was as if fear didn't exist in him." When Murphy finally leaped off the burning tank destroyer, the German attackers had pulled back. He had singlehandedly delayed their advance, allowing the rest of his unit to reorganize. Wounded in the leg, he still insisted on leading a counterattack. This single act of valor earned him the Medal of Honor, America's highest military decoration.

WOUNDS, MEDALS, AND A RETURN HOME

That day near Holtzwihr wasn't the only time Murphy displayed remarkable courage. He consistently led from the front in other battles, picking off enemy snipers, rescuing pinned-down allies, and volunteering for scouting missions in no-man's-land. By the end of the war, Audie Murphy had earned every major U.S. combat award available at the time, including the Distinguished Service Cross, two Silver Stars, and three Purple Hearts for wounds suffered in action. When Germany finally surrendered in May 1945, Murphy was a war hero at just 20 years old. However, his experiences had taken a toll. He lost friends, suffered physical injuries, and faced painful memories that would haunt him for the rest of his life. Returning home to a hero's welcome, he discovered that the war had changed him more than he ever expected.

In the years following World War II, Audie Murphy's fame spread nationwide. Newspapers ran headlines about this young Texan who had shown so much bravery. Hollywood producers, sensing a compelling story, invited Murphy to act in war movies. Reluctantly, he agreed, hoping it might give him enough income to support himself and his siblings. He appeared in several films, including "To Hell and Back," which was based on his autobiography. Though the thought of reliving those battles on screen was painful, he saw it as an opportunity to honor the friends he'd lost and share their stories.

People who worked with Murphy in Hollywood noticed he was a quiet and humble man, often more comfortable riding horses than attending glamorous parties. One producer commented, "Audie was a genuine hero, but he never bragged. The scars he carried were more than physical, and he struggled with them every day."

Despite the success in films, Murphy wrestled with what doctors would later call Post-Traumatic Stress Disorder (PTSD). Nightmares haunted his sleep. Sudden noises could make him jump. He spoke openly about these struggles at a time when few veterans received proper mental health support. By doing so, he helped pave the way for greater awareness of the invisible wounds many soldiers carry after war. He also used his celebrity to advocate for better treatment of returning veterans. Though he had found fame, he never forgot the ordinary GIs who had fought by his side. He wanted them to be remembered and cared for, insisting that bravery came in many forms—often from unsung heroes who never appeared in headlines.

Audie Murphy continued acting in Westerns and war films throughout the 1950s and 1960s. Tragically, he died in a plane crash in 1971 at the age of 45. When news of his death broke, tributes poured in from veterans, filmmakers, and everyday citizens who recalled his valor and humility. He was laid to rest at Arlington National Cemetery, where his grave remains one of the most visited sites—a silent tribute to a man who gave so much for his country.

On their own, one soldier can't transform the entire fate of a global conflict. But Audie Murphy's actions did boost morale among Allied forces. His successes, especially in battles across France, helped secure territories the Allies needed to push the Germans back. His legendary stand at Holtzwihr bought precious time for the Americans to regroup, preventing a possible breakthrough by the enemy. When ordinary soldiers heard about this quiet Texan who held off waves of attackers by himself, they felt renewed confidence in their own missions. Sometimes, a single act of courage can be a rallying cry for countless others.

More importantly, Murphy's story reminded the American public why these battles mattered. He hadn't been a general planning strategies from behind a desk; he was a young man from humble beginnings who sacrificed to protect freedom. The knowledge that such individuals existed bolstered the belief that the Allied cause was righteous and unstoppable.

Audie Murphy's life did not follow the typical path of a movie star or politician. He was, at heart, a farm boy turned reluctant warrior, drawn into global events by the necessity of survival and duty. That he emerged as America's most decorated soldier testifies to his unwavering resolve and skill under fire. The men who served alongside him still speak of his readiness to face danger, his calm under pressure, and his dedication to those he led. If you have courage, determination, and a desire to protect others, you can achieve incredible feats—even if you're small in stature or born into poverty. For a boy from rural Texas to transform into a national hero proves that real greatness often blossoms from the most unlikely seeds.

Meet America's most decorated WWII hero! Scan here to watch a quick, inspiring look at Audie Murphy's incredible bravery.

The Sandakan Rescuers

High in the lush jungles of Borneo, a tragic and heroic story unfolded during the final year of World War II. A group of prisoners of war (POWs), mostly Australians and some British, were forced by the occupying Japanese army to undertake a series of brutal marches that would later be remembered as the Sandakan Death Marches. Very few of these prisoners survived. Yet, amid fear and suffering, brave local villagers, tribal leaders, and resistance fighters risked everything to help these men. Their acts of kindness and courage saved lives and continue to inspire people today.

THE NIGHTMARE BEGINS

By 1945, the war in the Pacific had grown desperate for the Japanese forces. They occupied large parts of Southeast Asia, including North Borneo (what is now Sabah, Malaysia). In the town of Sandakan, the Japanese established a POW camp where captured soldiers were forced to work on building airstrips. Food was scarce, conditions were brutal, and many of the prisoners grew weak from hunger and illness. As the Allies gained ground in the region, the Japanese decided to move these POWs inland to prevent them from being freed. Over several months, they marched hundreds of men through dense rainforests, across rivers, and up steep mountain trails toward a remote area called Ranau. The marches were exhausting and often deadly. Anyone who fell behind risked being beaten or worse. A POW survivor, Warrant Officer Bill Moxham, once recalled, "We were all skin and bones, stumbling through the mud. I never knew if I'd see the next sunrise."

The local people living in the region were a diverse mix of communities. Some were farmers; others hunted in the rainforests for a living. Many belonged to indigenous tribes such as the Dusun, Murut, or Dayak peoples. They had little reason to trust the occupying Japanese soldiers, whose presence disrupted their way of life. Yet, these locals felt enormous sympathy for the starving prisoners who were marched past their villages. Despite the risks, countless villagers and tribespeople decided to help the POWs in whatever way they could. Some offered food—often just a handful of rice or a piece of dried fish. Others provided fresh water from the streams. A few even dared to hide escapees, guiding them through hidden jungle paths. Their compassion was remarkable, considering that if they were caught, they would suffer severe punishment from the Japanese army. An elderly villager named Wanita, who was a child at the time, described her family's decision to help, "My father saw the prisoners stumbling by. He told us, 'These men are in great pain. We must share what little we have.' We were afraid, but we couldn't just watch them suffer."

Beyond the villagers, there were also organized resistance fighters hidden in the jungles. These groups, sometimes aided by Allied intelligence units, kept track of Japanese troop movements and, when possible, sabotaged their plans. Hearing about the death marches, they focused on rescuing any POWs who managed to slip away from the main group. They hid the escapees in caves or in the thick undergrowth, smuggled them medicine, and helped them navigate the treacherous trails to safety. "Every time we found a sick or wounded prisoner, we knew it was a race against time. The jungle could hide us, but it could also swallow us if we weren't careful." Paul Basintal, a resistance member, said. Their efforts were incredibly dangerous. Japanese patrols scoured the forests, and the punishment for aiding prisoners was often death. Still, the rescuers pressed on, driven by the belief that every life saved was worth the risk.

THE FEW WHO ESCAPED

The Sandakan Death Marches proved to be among the worst atrocities committed in the Pacific theater of World War II. Out of more than 2,000 Allied prisoners who started the ordeal, only six survived to the end of the war—an almost unimaginable loss. But those six escaped, in large part, because of the heroism of local Borneo villagers and resistance fighters. One survivor, Keith Botterill, described how he was helped by a tribal family after fleeing into the jungle: "I could barely walk, and my friend was close to collapse. We came across a small hut where a family lived. Though frightened, they gave us rice and hid us under their floorboards when Japanese soldiers passed through." Another escapee, Owen Campbell, recalled how an older tribesman guided him across a river at night, using only moonlight to see. That man risked his life by assisting Campbell, but he did it anyway, simply stating, "A life is worth saving."

Helping the POWs was a simple matter of human compassion for many locals. Some never even learned the prisoners' names or where they were from. They only saw men desperately needing water, food, or a safe place to rest. Occasionally, they would offer secret signs to guide prisoners to hidden trails or safe spots to hide. Children sometimes acted as lookouts, quietly warning their parents if Japanese patrols approached. Women cooked extra rice, hoping it might sustain at least one hungry prisoner. Men scouted the hills at night to determine when it was safe to lead an escapee to the next hiding place. Each step required courage because the penalty for getting caught was severe.

In addition to saving lives, these villagers also bore witness to the brutal treatment the prisoners suffered. Some saw how exhausted POWs were beaten or left behind. Others discovered the heartbreak of those who could walk no farther and simply collapsed in the jungle. These terrible sights motivated the local people to do more, even if their resources were scarce. A local teacher, Mariam, wrote in her journal decades later, "I was only a teenager, but I remember how hollow the prisoners' eyes were. They had seen too much pain. We didn't have much, but we gave them hope." This generosity reminded everyone that even in the darkest times, kindness can flourish.

Not all rescues happened by chance. Occasionally, Allied planes dropped supplies or sent small teams of special operatives into the jungle. These agents contacted the local resistance groups, offering radios and medical kits. Together, they coordinated missions to evacuate the sickest prisoners. It was dangerous work for everyone involved. One Australian operative, Major Tom Harrisson, admired the bravery of the local helpers, saying, "They knew these jungles like the back of their hands, and they risked their lives to shelter foreigners they had never met. It was a form of courage the world should never forget." Though not every rescue mission succeeded, each effort raised the prisoners' chances of survival. Over time, the story of these clandestine rescues spread, inspiring hope among Allied soldiers still in Japanese captivity elsewhere.

LIGHT AT THE END OF THE TUNNEL

In August 1945, Japan officially surrendered, ending the war in the Pacific. By then, the Sandakan Death Marches had claimed nearly all the POWs. Those few survivors owed their lives to local villagers, tribal communities, and resistance fighters who offered them life-saving aid. When Allied troops finally arrived in North Borneo, they learned the full extent of the tragedy—and the heroism hidden within the jungles. Many villagers feared reprisal from any remaining Japanese soldiers, even after the surrender. But Allied forces assured them that their bravery would be recognized. Over time, word of the Borneo Death March

Rescuers spread to Australia and beyond, shining a light on the quiet sacrifices made by everyday people.

For years, the horrors of the Sandakan Death Marches were not widely known outside of Australia and Borneo. Some survivors were too traumatized to speak openly of their experiences. Others felt the world wouldn't understand such a grim story. Over time, however, historians uncovered more details, and the heroism of the local rescuers began to surface in documentaries, articles, and memorial ceremonies. In Borneo itself, families passed down stories of grandparents who shared the little food they had or guided exhausted men through the forest at night. Some villages set up small memorials, placing plaques or crosses where POWs had once collapsed. These quiet tributes served as a reminder that humanity can blossom even in the darkest jungles of war.

A few survivors later gave interviews in which they praised their rescuers. Keith Botterill never forgot the family who risked everything for him, stating,

> "They owed me nothing, but they treated me like kin. Without them, I wouldn't have lived."

Owen Campbell insisted that the real heroes were the villagers themselves:

> "We soldiers wore uniforms and carried a sense of duty. These people didn't have to help us, but they did anyway, with love in their hearts."

Such heartfelt words show how deeply these men appreciated the compassion strangers showed them. The efforts of the villagers and resistance fighters also provided valuable information about Japanese movements in the region, helping Allied forces plan future operations. By assisting the few prisoners who escaped, these rescuers ensured that the stories of cruelty on the Death Marches wouldn't remain hidden forever.

Every chapter in history has moments when people show extraordinary bravery. Still, the Borneo Death March Rescuers stand out for risking everything to assist strangers—prisoners of war they had never met. Their story proves that the human spirit can overcome even the terrors of war. They stayed true to values of kindness and compassion, reminding us that one small act of help can save a life. Although the Death Marches ended in heartbreak for many, the legacy of the rescuers shines brightly.

Today, memorials in Sabah honor those who perished in the Sandakan Death Marches and celebrate the local communities that offered help. Relatives of the rescuers still pass down stories, ensuring that the memory of their compassion doesn't fade. Historians and survivors' families work together to keep these events alive in the public mind. In their actions, we see how empathy can transcend fear, cruelty, and despair. Their story shows that real heroes are those who choose to act when it would be far easier to look away—and that, in doing so, they can change someone else's world forever.

Scan for a glimpse into genuine WWII diaries! *Though not from soldiers at Sandakan, these authentic entries reveal the bare-bones meals they survived on, the injuries they carried and their roiling emotions.*

The Battle of Britain

It was the summer of 1940, and the skies over England were about to become the world's most important battlefield. In just a few months, Great Britain had found itself facing a huge challenge. Almost all of Europe had fallen under Nazi Germany's control. France had surrendered, leaving Britain to stand alone against Adolf Hitler's powerful war machine. It was a frightening time, and the British knew that if the Nazis could not defeat the Royal Air Force (RAF), then perhaps there was still hope of stopping Hitler altogether.

WE SHALL FIGHT THEM

After the fall of France in June 1940, Adolf Hitler expected Britain to seek peace. But Prime Minister Winston Churchill vowed to fight on, no matter the cost. His stirring speeches echoed throughout the country. In one of them, he declared, "We shall fight on the beaches, we shall fight on the landing grounds, we shall fight in the fields and in the streets..." letting the British people know that surrender wasn't an option. To conquer Britain, the German Luftwaffe (their air force) needed to wipe out the RAF and gain control of the skies. If the Luftwaffe succeeded, Hitler could launch a major invasion of the British Isles, code-named "Operation Sea Lion." On the other side, if the RAF held strong, Germany would be forced to postpone or abandon its plan. The fate of the war depended on this aerial struggle: The Battle of Britain.

At the heart of Britain's air defense strategy was Air Chief Marshal Hugh Dowding, a thoughtful and serious leader who had spent years organizing a system that combined early-warning radar stations, spotters, and fighter squadrons. Under Dowding's direction, the RAF created a network of radar posts along the coast. Whenever enemy planes appeared, operators tracked their movements and telephoned

RAF headquarters. Quickly, fighter pilots would scramble into the skies to meet the threat. This was a new way of fighting. In earlier wars, armies clashed on vast fields. Now, the battle would be decided by the speed of airplanes and the alertness of radar operators. Dowding calmly explained to his pilots, "We have one job: defend our island. Remember what you fight for, and let that guide you."

The RAF squadrons were made up of young pilots from many backgrounds—some were British, others had fled occupied countries like Poland or Czechoslovakia. Eager to fight the Nazis, they brought their own determination and skill. Many were barely out of their teens. They lived in simple barracks, waiting each day for the call to scramble. When the alarm sounded, they ran to their sleek Hurricane or Spitfire fighters, engines roaring as they sped into the skies. One RAF pilot, Alan Deere, wrote in his diary, "Whenever I took off, I felt both fear and excitement. I never knew if I'd see nightfall, yet I couldn't wait to challenge the German bombers." Far above the British countryside, aerial dogfights raged. German planes flew in large formations, escorted by fighter planes called Messerschmitts. The RAF pilots often had to climb thousands of feet within minutes. They zoomed through clouds, adrenaline pumping, guns at the ready.

Early on, the Germans seemed to have the upper hand. They had more planes and experienced bomber crews. Many German pilots were battle-hardened from earlier campaigns in Poland and France. Their high command believed Britain could be crushed in just a few weeks of intense bombing. However, they underestimated the RAF's determination and the importance of the relatively new radar technology. While the Luftwaffe regularly bombed airfields and radar stations, they found themselves challenged by the quick RAF response. Whenever a German squadron tried to surprise the Brits, they discovered Spitfires and Hurricanes already climbing to meet them. Still, the Luftwaffe kept coming, attacking day after day in the summer and early autumn of 1940.

July turned to August, and August to September, and the skies seemed constantly filled with aircraft. British ground crews worked through nights to patch up bullet holes, re-fuel planes, and ready the next morning's sorties. The pilots would catch a few hours of sleep, always listening for the shrill ring of the telephone alert. Sometimes, they'd scramble three or four times a day. In the thick of the fighting, Squadron Leader Douglas Bader, a famous pilot who had lost both legs in a flying accident before the war, led formations with fearless enthusiasm. He once said, "Don't listen to the man who says you can't do it. He's the one who can't." Despite his disability, he became an inspiration to other pilots, proving that a strong will could overcome almost any obstacle. Pilots like Eric Lock, the RAF's top-scoring fighter ace during the Battle of Britain, shot down multiple German planes in a single day. Others engaged in harrowing dogfights where a split-second decision could mean life or death. No matter how many missions he flew, each pilot knew that tomorrow's battle might be his last.

THE BLITZ

As the Luftwaffe struggled to defeat the RAF in direct combat, Hitler ordered a new tactic: the bombing of British cities. In particular, the capital city of London became a target. This phase, known as the Blitz, saw German bombers crossing the Channel by night, raining destruction on factories, homes, and railways. Civilians sought refuge in bomb shelters or underground train stations. Though the Blitz was terrifying, it unintentionally relieved pressure on RAF airfields. With fewer attacks on their runways and radar stations, British fighters had a chance to recover. Moreover, the bombing of cities enraged the British people, strengthening their resolve rather than breaking it. Families huddled together in basements, determined not to let fear rule them. One Londoner recalled, "We heard the explosions all night, but we sang songs to keep our spirits up. If they wanted to scare us, it wasn't working." In time, the RAF soared back into the skies. Spitfires and Hurricanes intercepted bombers heading for London, braving flak and enemy fire to protect the city below.

By September, it became clear that the Luftwaffe hadn't gained air superiority. The RAF was battered but still fighting fiercely. On August 20, 1940, Winston Churchill delivered a speech praising the pilots who defended Britain. It included the famous line, "Never in the field of human conflict was so much owed by so many to so few." Ever since the RAF pilots of that time have been honored as "The Few." They were a handful of defenders who saved countless lives. When young pilots heard those words, they felt both pride and a heavy responsibility. They knew the survival of their country—and possibly the free world—rested on their wings and their willingness to take incredible risks.

Slowly but surely, the Luftwaffe's losses piled up. German commanders realized they couldn't afford to lose more planes and crews at the rate the RAF was shooting them down. Hitler postponed his plans to invade Britain. While bombing raids continued, the Germans no longer held hopes of crushing the RAF outright. The Battle of Britain, which lasted from July to October 1940, ended with Britain still uninvaded and undefeated. A German pilot, Adolf Galland, reportedly told his superiors that what the Luftwaffe really needed was "a squadron of Spitfires," acknowledging the exceptional performance of Britain's aircraft. Though it was an exaggeration, it showed genuine respect for the skill of British pilots and the effectiveness of their planes.

LIFE AFTER THE BATTLE

After the Battle of Britain, those who flew in it were never quite the same. Some had earned fame as fighter aces, others quietly returned to regular duty, and many had lost friends in the fighting. The people of Britain viewed them with immense gratitude. Memorials appeared in towns and villages, bearing the names of young men who never came home. In newspapers, the pilots were hailed as heroes. But even outside the cockpit, the lesson of the battle was clear: a determined group, well-prepared and bravely led, could stand against a seemingly unstoppable foe. Each pilot's story became a thread in a larger tapestry of courage.

Why was the Battle of Britain so important? For one thing, it was the first significant defeat the Germans suffered in World War II. Until then, the Nazi blitzkrieg (lightning war) had knocked down every country it faced. Britain's victory proved that Hitler's forces were not invincible. The RAF's success also gave hope to occupied nations in Europe. If Britain could hold out, perhaps one day, those under Nazi rule might be freed. This battle also kept Britain in the war as a vital base for the Allies. If the Germans had taken Britain, the history of WWII might have unfolded very differently. Instead, Britain became a launching pad for future Allied operations, including the eventual D-Day landings that would liberate Western Europe in 1944. Most of all, the Battle of Britain inspired people worldwide to believe that courage and steadfastness could overcome tyranny. Countless schoolchildren in Britain—and later in many Allied nations—grew up hearing the story of "The Few," those heroic pilots who refused to surrender the skies.

The men and women who fought in or supported the Battle of Britain taught us that teamwork, technology, and bravery can turn the tide of a war. The radar stations, ground crews, and fighter pilots formed a chain of defense that the Luftwaffe just couldn't break. Their victory showed how one small island could stand firm against a mightier enemy. In the years after the war, Winston Churchill's words continued to echo. Historians wrote books about the pilot aces, the creation of radar, and the resilience of ordinary people under the Blitz. Pilot Richard Hillary wrote in his memoir, "When I climbed into my Spitfire, I felt a strange calm. Fear came later, but in that moment, all that mattered was defending my home." That spirit of defending what was cherished—freedom, families, and a sense of right—defined the Battle of Britain.

A LEGACY OF HOPE AND DETERMINATION

In the end, the Battle of Britain wasn't merely an exchange of gunfire in the sky. It was a clash of wills, where a smaller force stood up to a powerful aggressor. The best technology alone wasn't enough; the entire nation played a role, from the pilots who braved daily dogfights to the civilians who kept life going despite bombs falling on their cities. Those who lived through it would never forget the days when the sky thundered with engines or the nights filled with searchlights and the crack of anti-aircraft guns. But they emerged, knowing that they had stood firm and defended their small island from a great threat. And for the rest of the world, the lesson was clear: even when odds seem impossible, courage can make you victorious.

THE MOST INSPIRING WORLD WAR 2 STORIES

Witness the skies roar to life! Scan and see the epic Battle of Britain in a thrilling 90-second animation.

Glenn Miller and The Power of Music

In 1942, the world was in turmoil as the war entered its third year. People struggled to survive, and morale was at an all-time low. Amid this uncertainty, one man believed music could bring hope and relief to all who heard it: Alton Glenn Miller, an American jazz musician and bandleader. By forming the Army Air Force Band, Miller demonstrated that even in the darkest times, music could uplift spirits, inspire courage, and evoke memories of simpler, happier days.

Glenn Miller initally tried to join the Navy, hoping to form a band that would play on battleships and in naval camps. But the Navy turned him down, feeling unsure about how to use a big-band musician. Not one to give up easily, Miller approached the Army Air Forces. Eventually, they recognized the value of his proposal. It wasn't just about music —it was about lifting morale, keeping soldiers' spirits high, and reminding them why they fought in the first place.

INSTRUMENTAL IN BATTLE

Soon after, Miller received permission to organize an Army Air Force Band. He traded in his stylish suit for a crisp military uniform, and by the summer of 1943, he wore captain's bars on his shoulders. His mission: bring a sense of joy and unity to the war effort through music. He once said to a friend, "I'm not here to make a million dollars. I'm here to share music with our boys who need it more than ever."

Bringing together skilled musicians from across the Armed Forces was no easy task. Many talented players were already scattered across training camps or stationed overseas. Miller sent out word that he needed trombonists, saxophonists, drummers—everyone who could contribute to a first-rate big band. Little by little, a group of dedicated musicians assembled. Some had been part of swing bands back home; others had performed in local orchestras or school jazz groups. All shared a passion for music and a willingness to serve. One saxophonist, Sergeant Jerry Yelverton, later recalled his excitement at joining Miller's group: "We'd been playing in different bands, but now we could play under Glenn Miller himself. It felt like an honor, and we hoped our music would bring joy to thousands."

A NEW MILITARY MISSION

The newly formed Army Air Force Band didn't resemble a traditional military band. Instead, it reflected Miller's trademark style—saxophones, trumpets, trombones, a rhythm section—capable of playing both peppy swing numbers and sentimental ballads. Band members still had to follow military protocol: saluting officers, standing in formation, and wearing regulation uniforms. But when rehearsal began, the familiar warmth of swing music replaced strict drills. The band's purpose was clear: entertain troops, perform on radio broadcasts, and strengthen morale. The Army saw the band as a crucial tool. Soldiers far from home needed something to remind them of the life they were fighting to preserve. And Glenn Miller's music, with its bright horns and toe-tapping rhythm, seemed the perfect choice.

During 1943, Miller and his band toured around the United States, playing in various military camps, hospitals, and radio stations. At each stop, soldiers gathered for a chance to hear a live performance of the famous tunes they knew from back home. Whether it was the energetic "In the Mood" or the romantic "Moonlight Serenade," the music stirred up memories of family dances and weekend outings. For a while, the soldiers could forget the grim reality of war. Carlton Price, young American private, recalled listening to the band at an airfield in Texas: "My unit was about to ship out. Hearing Glenn Miller perform that night made us feel less scared. It was like a small piece of home followed us wherever we went." Such comments motivated the band to keep going. They understood that each concert gave the troops a brief escape from the tensions of training and deployment.

By mid-1944, the Allies had landed in Normandy, France, pushing slowly toward Germany. Large numbers of American service members were now stationed in England, preparing for further operations. Glenn Miller felt that his place was with them. He requested permission to move his band overseas so they could perform for the soldiers directly on the European front.

The Army agreed, and soon, Miller and his musicians sailed across the Atlantic. Arriving in London, they set up base in a city still subject to German bombings. Almost immediately, they began broadcasting on the radio as part of the Allied Expeditionary Forces Programme. These broadcasts weren't only for Americans; they also reached Allied troops from other nations, and sometimes even ordinary British civilians tuned in.

The band traveled around England, performing in hangars, assembly halls, and sometimes outdoors on makeshift stages. They'd lug heavy instruments on and off trucks, set up quickly, and play for crowds of uniformed men and women. Soldiers, nurses, and local townspeople came together to enjoy the music. It reminded everyone that while the conflict raged on, humanity hadn't lost its heart. Amid these travels, the band also kept up a busy schedule of radio recordings. Programs like "Glenn Miller's Midnight Serenade" or "AEF Band Show" brought joy to Americans, Britons, and others fighting the Axis. Glenn Miller, baton in hand, would stand at the center, guiding his ensemble with careful precision. During breaks, he chatted with troops, asking about their hometowns and loved ones. British Major Ian MacGregor, summed it up best by saying, "In those anxious months, nothing lifted spirits more than Glenn Miller's music. It was like an antidote to fear."

GONE BUT NOT FORGOTTEN

Then came December 15, 1944. Glenn Miller boarded a small plane in England, bound for Paris, where his band was scheduled to play a Christmas concert. The weather was poor—cold, foggy, and treacherous for flying. Miller, the pilot, and one passenger took off, but they never arrived in Paris. The plane vanished over the English Channel, leaving no trace behind. News of Miller's disappearance stunned not just the band, but the entire Allied community. Hope lingered briefly that he might have survived a crash, but days turned to weeks with no word. Eventually, authorities declared him missing and presumed dead. The impact on morale was profound. Many cried, realizing that the man who had kept so many spirits high had lost his own life in the line of duty.

Despite the tragedy, the Army Air Force Band continued its mission. Miller would have wanted the music to go on. Under the leadership of other members, the band stayed together, performing for troops across liberated areas of France and Belgium. They also contributed to broadcasts meant to reassure Allied forces that the fight for freedom continued. Each show now carried added meaning. Band members felt they were playing not just for the soldiers but also in honor of Glenn Miller's memory. The cheerful tunes served as a testament to his belief that music could lift hearts even in the darkest times. "It wasn't easy without him. But every time we played, we felt Glenn in the notes. We owed it to him—and to the troops—to keep that spirit alive," said Sergeant Yelverton.

While Glenn Miller and the Army Air Force Band didn't win battles directly, they boosted morale, and in war, morale matters greatly. Soldiers who heard beloved tunes felt more connected to home. That emotional support made them stronger, more determined to keep going. When people are reminded of what they're fighting for—family, friendship, freedom—they fight with greater resolve. The idea of an entire nation tapping its feet to the same songs created unity at a time when unity was crucial. Glenn Miller's desire to serve his country by giving people hope turned him into a different sort of hero: not on the battlefield but in the hearts of those who listened.

A LASTING INSPIRATION

When the war ended in 1945, the memory of Glenn Miller and his Army Air Force Band endured. Musicians returning home told stories about lugging instruments across muddy fields, playing on battered stages, and seeing tears of happiness in the eyes of weary soldiers. Many credited Miller with showing how the power of melody could unite people. A generation grew up on the warm sounds of big-band swing, associating it with images of victory parades and emotional reunions. In later years, historians documented Miller's influence on military music programs. The concept of using entertainment to support troop morale became standard practice. Today, whether it's a rock concert in a desert base or a comedy tour on an aircraft carrier, the seeds of that tradition were planted by Glenn Miller's Army Air Force Band. So, when you hear old recordings of "In the Mood" or "Moonlight Serenade," know that these tunes aren't just catchy melodies from long ago. They're symbols of hope and resolve, shaped by a man who believed music could bring light to the darkness of war. Glenn Miller and the Army Air Force Band showed that, even amid gunfire and chaos, a well-played note can resonate across oceans and generations—reminding us that the best of humanity endures, guided by harmony and heart.

BLOOMLIT PRESS

Hear the music that boosted spirits on the front lines! Scan here to listen to one of Captain Glenn Miller's rousing WWII recordings.

The Ghost Army

Far from the front lines of WWII, a mysterious group of American soldiers fought a very different kind of battle—one of trickery and illusions. They were the 23rd Headquarters Special Troops, better known as the Ghost Army. Their job was not to fire weapons or charge into battle but to create convincing fakes—inflatable tanks, phony radio signals, and other deceptions—so the enemy would be fooled about where and how the Allies planned to strike next. Because this unit was so unusual, it needed soldiers who thought outside the box. Some were famous artists or fashion designers; others were painters or theater set designers. Among them was Bill Blass, who later became a famous fashion designer, and Ellsworth Kelly, who would gain recognition as a major artist. At first, they went through basic Army training just like every other recruit—learning to march, salute, and shoot. But soon after, they were pulled aside and handed top-secret orders.

BLOW-UP TANKS

One of the Ghost Army's main tactics involved inflatable vehicles: tanks, jeeps, artillery, and even airplanes made of rubberized canvas. These dummies were easy to transport. With a few portable air pumps, a handful of soldiers could set up dozens of "vehicles" in a matter of hours. Seen from a distance—or through binoculars—these blow-up tanks looked genuine. Enemy spy planes taking photos or ground troops scouting from afar would report a large Allied force, never guessing most of it was just air-filled fabric. A soldier named John Jarvie wrote in a letter home, "You'd be amazed how lifelike our dummy tanks appear—until a breeze comes along and they wobble like balloons at a parade."

Visual illusions weren't the only trick. The Ghost Army also became masters of sound deception. They recorded the rumble of tanks, the clank of machinery, and the echo of marching feet onto large phonograph discs or magnetic tapes. Then, using powerful loudspeakers hidden behind trees or bushes, they blasted these recordings at night. German listening posts would hear what sounded like thousands of soldiers gathering. In reality, there might be fewer than a hundred men, each working carefully to stage an elaborate show. On one occasion, the unit's sound team set up near a quiet road in France. As soon as darkness fell, they played the roar of engines and shouted commands in various languages, making the enemy believe an entire Allied division was approaching. Meanwhile, the real troops were slipping away to mount a surprise attack somewhere else.

During WWII, radio waves crackled with messages back and forth. The Ghost Army had expert radio operators who knew how the Germans eavesdropped on Allied communications. These operators sent out phony messages in code, pretending to be the radio operators of real units. For instance, if the 75th Infantry Division was moving north, the Ghost Army might broadcast misleading signals suggesting the 75th was staying put or heading west. German intelligence could intercept these signals and make decisions based on false clues. All of this required planning and skill. The operators had to mimic different communication styles and keep track of what real divisions were up to, so their fake messages would sound authentic. Sergeant Larry Decrow from The Ghost Army, later explained the meticulous attention to detail the showed, "We had to know how each division's operator typically spoke—what phrases he used, how quickly he tapped Morse code. We replicated those tiny details to avoid suspicion."

Some Ghost Army members were professional painters and sculptors. They painted entire backdrops, building elaborate illusions of campsites and tank formations. They'd prop up fake laundry on clotheslines to suggest a big group was staying in the area. They created makeshift roads, scuffing the ground to mimic heavy tire tracks. When enemy planes flew overhead, they'd see what looked like a full-scale base. From the ground, it might even smell real if the Ghost Army decided to light small campfires or cook meals to sell the deception further. One soldier recalled how, before an operation, they spent hours brushing footprints into muddy fields so it appeared hundreds of men had trampled the ground. Every detail, no matter how small, could convince an enemy spy that a large force was present.

CHASING PHANTOMS

The Ghost Army's illusions were used in at least 20 major operations across Europe, from Normandy after D-Day to the Rhine River in Germany. Their missions were so secret that many regular Allied troops nearby had no idea the "tank division" camped next door wasn't real. The risk was huge: if German troops discovered the truth, the Ghost Army's soldiers—armed mostly with paint and inflatable props—would be in grave danger. When they were in the thick of it, some worried the ruse was too good. Alan Johnson, an artist in the unit, admitted, "Sometimes, we'd inflate the decoys and think, 'This is so convincing, we're fooling our own guys, too.' But that was exactly the point."

Because deception often required the Ghost Army to be close to enemy lines, these creative soldiers sometimes found themselves under fire. German patrols might stumble onto an inflatable tank that wasn't fully inflated or a speaker truck broadcasting recorded noises. The Ghost Army had to work quickly, setting up their illusions, then slipping away before anyone got suspicious. A few times, they found themselves in skirmishes, forced to grab rifles and defend themselves until reinforcements arrived. Despite the danger, their illusions saved countless lives. By diverting German troops away from real Allied divisions, they prevented many battles that could have ended in heavy casualties.

One Army officer later remarked that for every Ghost Army mission, the number of Allied soldiers placed at risk elsewhere dropped dramatically because the Germans were chasing phantoms, not real forces.

The Ghost Army's tactics felt like Hollywood magic. Indeed, the unit often borrowed ideas from movie set designers. They understood that war is sometimes a game of illusions—if you could make the enemy believe you had more men and equipment than you actually did, you could force them to change their plans. For example, if you convinced them you were building up troops in the north, they might move their divisions there, leaving the south vulnerable to a real attack. "We used every theatrical trick in the book—lighting, props, costumes, and stage effects—but instead of entertaining an audience, we were fooling the enemy," Private Tony Rossi said,

The Ghost Army never marched in grand parades or captured headlines like the infantry divisions or tank battalions. Their success depended on secrecy, so few knew about their achievements until decades after the war. Yet historians agree that their work significantly helped the Allied cause, especially after the D-Day landings when the Allies needed every advantage to outsmart German defenses. Their illusions allowed real soldiers to move unseen. They also confused high-ranking German officers, who often made costly mistakes by sending reinforcements to the wrong locations. In the chaos of wartime, these illusions could shift the balance of a battle. Though it's impossible to count the exact number of lives the Ghost Army saved, many who studied its operations say that without these deceptions, some Allied offensives would have faced far more resistance and suffering.

A BATTLE OF IMAGINATION

These soldiers proved that brains and clever ideas could be just as effective as bullets. They took a risk by standing on the front lines armed with illusions rather than heavy artillery, all for the goal of ending the war sooner and with fewer casualties. Their belief that imagination can be a powerful weapon is what truly makes The Ghost Army stand out as secret heroes of WWII.

Years later, when their missions were finally declassified, many Americans were surprised to learn that artists, stage designers, and advertising pros had played such a key role in beating the Nazis. The story of the Ghost Army has since fascinated people worldwide, showing that art and strategy can blend in unexpected ways.

After the war, the soldiers in the Ghost Army went back to their lives. Some became famous painters and designers; others returned to regular jobs, never mentioning the top-secret operations they'd taken part in. The U.S. Army kept details of their work under wraps for decades, concerned that the deception tactics might be useful in future conflicts. Only in recent years have historians uncovered documents and interviewed surviving members to piece together the full story. For most of their lives, these veterans never sought recognition. They quietly carried the memory of nights inflating tanks by moonlight, or days spent blasting the sounds of convoys through hidden speakers. Many felt proud, knowing their illusions had helped bring a quicker end to a terrible war.

Their legacy lives on as an inspiration to think creatively, work together, and never underestimate the power of a clever idea. As Colonel Harry Reeder, who served in the unit, said, "It was a battle of imagination more than firepower." A battle they most certainly won.

John F. Kennedy and PT-109

In the dark waters of the Pacific Ocean during World War II, a young American naval officer named John Fitzgerald Kennedy found himself in a life-or-death struggle. What happened next would become one of the most inspiring stories of bravery and leadership to emerge from the war.

A FUTURE LEADER GOES TO WAR

John F. Kennedy, often called Jack by his friends and family, was born into a prominent American family in 1917. His father, Joseph Kennedy, wanted all his children to excel in whatever they did. Jack grew up loving history and eventually studied at Harvard University. When the United States entered World War II after the attack on Pearl Harbor, Jack—despite struggling with health issues—insisted on joining the Navy. He trained for the Patrol Torpedo (PT) service, a demanding role that required young officers to command small, fast boats used for daring nighttime attacks against larger enemy ships.

PT-109 was part of Motor Torpedo Boat Squadron Two, stationed in the Solomon Islands in the South Pacific, where heavy fighting raged between the Allies and the Japanese forces. PT-109 was a slender wooden boat around 80 feet long, armed with four torpedo tubes, a few machine guns, and a crew of about a dozen men. Because the boat was made mostly of plywood, it was quick and nimble on the water. However, it offered very little protection if it ever got hit by enemy gunfire. Life on board could be uncomfortable. The Pacific heat felt stifling, and supplies were scarce. But the men worked together, forming a close bond. They respected Kennedy's calm approach under pressure. One crew member, Machinist's Mate Patrick McMahon, said later, "He took care of us, kept us all focused, and led by example." Kennedy learned each man's strengths and how to boost their morale.

In quiet moments, they would laugh, swap stories, and dream of going home.

THE COLLISION

On the night of August 1, 1943, Kennedy and his crew embarked on a mission to intercept Japanese ships slipping through nearby waters. In the darkness, PT-109 slowly cruised, hoping to catch enemy vessels off guard. However, the black sky offered almost no visibility. Around 2:00 AM, while most of the crew stayed alert at their stations, a sudden, looming shape emerged from the night: a Japanese destroyer named Amagiri. Before anyone could react, the massive enemy ship slammed into PT-109, cutting the smaller boat in half. The force of the impact ignited a fierce explosion and scattered debris. Flames lit the surface of the water. Two of Kennedy's crew were killed instantly, and others were thrown into the ocean. In a single heartbeat, their mission turned into a struggle for survival.

With the boat destroyed, the survivors clung to floating wreckage. Fuel spread across the waves, making the water shine with a ghostly sheen. Some men were injured or badly burned. Kennedy checked on each one, making sure they remained calm. As an officer, he felt it was his duty to keep everyone together, even though the group had no food, limited water, and no way to send a radio signal for help. In the chaos, Pat McMahon—badly burned—struggled to stay afloat. Seeing this, Kennedy grabbed him by his life vest and began to tow him. Because McMahon was so weak, Kennedy clamped the vest strap in his teeth and swam, determined not to leave a single crewmate behind.

At daylight, Kennedy spotted a small island several miles away. Though it offered no guarantee of rescue, it was their only chance to find shelter. Gathering his men, he directed them to start swimming or paddling on whatever debris they could hold onto. The ocean currents proved strong, but eventually they reached the shoreline. Exhausted, they collapsed on the sandy beach. While the group rested, Kennedy set out to explore the island. It was uninhabited—no signs of fresh water or local villagers who might help. As the sun beat down, thirst became a growing concern. Kennedy, refusing to give up, told his men they would have to push on to another island or risk dying of dehydration. One of the crew, Raymond Albert, later said, "Our spirits were low, but the skipper kept us moving. He refused to lose hope."

THE BRAVE SWIM FOR HELP

That night, Kennedy slipped back into the water to look for a better island. He swam through miles of open ocean, scanning the darkness for any sign of rescue. At times, the fear of sharks weighed on him, but he pushed those thoughts aside. After hours, he discovered another small island, also lacking supplies. Yet he refused to give in. He swam back to his crew, guiding them across the waters in the following days, doing everything possible to keep them alive.

Eventually, they reached an island with a few coconuts and some hope of rescue. Kennedy and another crewmember carved a message into a coconut shell, reading:

"NAURO ISL... COMMANDER... NATIVE KNOWS POS'IT... HE CAN PILOT... 11 ALIVE... NEED SMALL BOAT... KENNEDY."

This coconut would become famous as a symbol of their survival. Kennedy entrusted it to two friendly islanders from the Solomon Islands—Biuku Gasa and Eroni Kumana—who happened upon the stranded crew. These men bravely paddled their canoe through dangerous waters to deliver the message to the nearest Allied base.

Thanks to the heroic efforts of Gasa and Kumana, word reached a nearby Australian coastwatcher named Reginald Evans. He, in turn, organized a rescue. On August 8, a small boat arrived to pick up Kennedy and his crew. Despite the ordeal, all the survivors—except for the two men lost in the collision—were safe. McMahon, who'd nearly drowned, later remarked, "Without Jack pulling me, I never would have made it." This rescue was a triumph of determination and teamwork. Kennedy's leadership shone through: he had kept the survivors united and used every ounce of energy to find help. He refused to abandon anyone, risking his own life multiple times.

Even after this close call, Kennedy didn't ask for a transfer away from the frontline. Instead, he took command of a different PT boat and resumed dangerous missions in the Solomons. His injuries, including a chronic back problem, grew worse, but he continued to serve until doctors insisted he leave. Years later, he would receive the Navy and Marine Corps Medal for his actions and the Purple Heart for his wounds.

Though this was only a small chapter in the vast war, the PT-109 incident captured public attention back in the United States. Newspapers reported on how the son of a prominent family had nearly died saving his men. Kennedy, modest about the event, often said, "It was involuntary. They sank my boat." Yet to his crew, he had shown extraordinary bravery and loyalty, qualities that would later define his future.

LEGACY

After the war, John F. Kennedy returned to the U.S., eventually embarking on a political career. Elected as President in 1960, he carried the lessons from his time in the Navy—courage under pressure, loyalty to his team, and an unshakable belief in public service. When he was sworn into office, he famously said, "Ask not what your country can do for you—ask what you can do for your country." Some say this spirit was forged in part by those harrowing days after PT-109 went down.

Decades later, Patrick McMahon said in an interview, "The rest of the world came to know him as President, but to us, he was the man who wouldn't leave anyone behind."

The coconut shell Kennedy used to send his message became an enduring symbol. He kept it in the Oval Office as a paperweight during his presidency, a reminder that a single bold action can stand between life and death. For many Americans, that battered coconut showed how resourcefulness and courage could shine through even in dire circumstances.

By refusing to give up, John F. Kennedy and the crew of PT-109 fueled hope at a time when the world desperately needed it. Their actions helped shape future events and left a powerful example for us all: that in the face of danger, leadership with heart can guide us to safety—and sometimes, to the pages of history.

The Siege of Bastogne

In December of 1944, a bitterly cold winter gripped the forests of Belgium. Snow covered the ground, and a piercing wind chilled soldiers to the bone. Although many believed the war in Europe was winding down, Nazi Germany launched a surprise attack through the dense Ardennes region. Allied forces scrambled to hold their positions, and in the middle of it all, the 101st Airborne Division found itself surrounded in a small Belgian town called Bastogne. Cut off from reinforcements, short on supplies, and facing freezing temperatures, these soldiers refused to surrender—and their determination became one of the most inspiring stories of World War II.

Earlier that month, the Allied armies had been pushing into western Germany, expecting the war to end soon. American troops took time to celebrate Christmas in their camps, though they remained watchful. Unexpectedly, on December 16, 1944, the Germans launched a massive counterattack, later known as the Battle of the Bulge. Tanks and infantry punched through thinly defended American lines, creating a giant "bulge" in the Allied front.

The 101st Airborne Division, also called the "Screaming Eagles," had been resting after fierce fighting in the Netherlands. Suddenly, they received urgent orders to move to Bastogne, a crossroads town in Belgium that the Allies could not afford to lose. Those roads were vital for moving tanks, trucks, and supplies. If the Germans captured Bastogne, they could rush deeper into Allied territory.

RACE TO BASTOGNE

The 101st Airborne piled into trucks and rumbled down icy roads. Many of these paratroopers had lost most of their winter gear during earlier missions, so they wore only thin jackets, some still tattered. They arrived in Bastogne on December 19, just ahead of the fast-advancing German columns.

Brigadier General Anthony McAuliffe assumed command in Bastogne. He immediately assigned units to defend the perimeter of the town. Soldiers dug foxholes in the frozen earth, while others set up machine guns behind piles of rubble. Civilians watched nervously from their windows. The temperature dropped even further, and snow began falling in steady flurries. One paratrooper, Private Arthur Riley, recalled, "We had no clue we'd be surrounded. We just knew the Germans were coming fast, and we had to hold on to Bastogne. It was do-or-die, and we were freezing."

By December 21, the German forces had completed a ring around Bastogne. Seven main roads led into the town, but all of them fell under enemy control. With supplies cut off, the 101st Airborne had to ration every round of ammunition, every meal, and every blanket. Even medical supplies ran short, leaving wounded soldiers with few painkillers or bandages. Trucks couldn't get through, and the overcast skies prevented most Allied planes from dropping supplies. Though conditions were dire, General McAuliffe and his officers boosted morale by reminding the men that their job was to hold, no matter what. The paratroopers were trained to fight in tough situations. They had already proven themselves in battles like Normandy and Operation Market Garden. Now, they braced themselves for a different kind of battle—a harsh siege with relentless artillery barrages, patrols, and nighttime attacks. "We'd been in rough spots before, but Bastogne was something else. We faced cold, hunger, and a huge enemy force. It tested our limits like never before," Sergeant Jim Martin later said.

THE BATTLE IN THE SNOW

As German tanks rolled closer, the men of the 101st dug deeper trenches. Fighting often broke out at dawn or dusk, with short, brutal clashes in the pine forests. The paratroopers carefully conserved bullets, firing only when absolutely necessary. German artillery shells rained down on the town, creating deep craters in the streets. Meanwhile, the wounded filled makeshift hospitals in basements and churches. Without adequate medical supplies, doctors and medics did their best, sometimes using torn-up clothes as bandages. Yet the 101st refused to let the hardships break them. They shared blankets, told jokes in hushed voices, and even sang Christmas carols in the rubble, trying to keep their spirits alive. When the weather cleared for a bit, Allied planes risked flying over Bastogne, dropping small bundles of supplies. Men scrambled to gather these precious crates, which contained desperately needed food, medicine, and ammunition. Many called these resupply missions "angels from the sky."

THE GERMAN DEMAND

By December 22, the German commanders surrounding Bastogne felt sure the Americans had no chance. Confident in their advantage, they sent a group of soldiers under a white flag to deliver a written demand for surrender to General McAuliffe. They expected him to see reason. After all, the 101st Airborne was outnumbered, cut off, and facing exhaustion.

But the 101st had other plans. When McAuliffe read the surrender demand, he famously exclaimed, "Aw, nuts!" That one word became a symbol of defiance. Soon after, he dictated an official reply to the German officers: simply, "NUTS!" In plain language, it meant the

Americans had no intention of surrendering. Years later, McAuliffe explained, "We were determined to hold Bastogne no matter how bad it got. The men understood that giving in wasn't an option. We were fighting for each other and for the entire Allied cause."

Infuriated by McAuliffe's response, the Germans intensified their attacks. Soldiers from the 101st fought from house to house, street to street. Snow continued to fall, making it hard to see more than a few yards ahead. Temperatures plummeted below freezing, sometimes dipping near zero degrees Fahrenheit. Still, the paratroopers clung to their positions, even when their boots froze or their breath turned to ice crystals on their collars.

To keep each other alive, they shared body heat and what little food remained. Some units ate the same rations for days, scrounging for any scraps they could find. At times, German tanks came so close that American bazookas had to aim at point-blank range. Despite the overwhelming force, the 101st refused to back down.

December 25 arrived with no holiday celebration for the besieged men. Instead, they spent most of Christmas Day repelling waves of German soldiers. Yet, they found small ways to mark the day. A few troopers fashioned a tiny Christmas tree from pine branches and decorated it with cartridge casings. Others scribbled letters home, not knowing if they'd ever get mailed.

In one corner of the town, Father Sampson, a military chaplain, held a simple service in the ruins of a church. Paratroopers listened quietly as he offered prayers for peace and the hope of rescue. Some men cried softly, missing their families more than ever. Sergeant Martin recalled, "It was the saddest, coldest Christmas I ever knew. But we held onto a shred of faith that we weren't forgotten."

HELP FINALLY ARRIVES

On December 26, the sound of distant artillery changed in tone. Something was happening outside the German encirclement. As the day wore on, scouts reported that General George S. Patton's Third Army was advancing toward Bastogne from the south, fighting fiercely to break through the enemy lines. The men of the 101st listened anxiously, hoping to see American tanks rolling in.

By late afternoon, Patton's forward units smashed through and reached the outskirts of Bastogne. Cheers erupted among the paratroopers and the townspeople. After nearly a week of being trapped, relief had arrived! Though the Germans still fought hard, they could no longer maintain the siege. The 101st was battered but unbroken. Their stand at Bastogne became legendary.

The defense of Bastogne helped stall the German offensive during the Battle of the Bulge. By denying the enemy a key crossroads, the 101st and other Allied units prevented the Germans from rushing deeper into Allied lines. Within weeks, the tide of the battle turned. The Allies pushed the German forces back, eventually restoring the front and continuing their drive toward Germany.

The ordeal in Bastogne also gave a huge boost to Allied morale. Word spread quickly of how a handful of paratroopers, short on supplies and freezing in subzero weather, had refused to surrender. Newspapers and radio broadcasts praised the men of the 101st. Civilians saw them as symbols of courage and determination. One French civilian who witnessed the siege later said, "We thought the Americans would break, but they never did. Their spirit was incredible."

Their bravery influenced future military strategies, too. Officers studied how a small, well-trained force could hold off a larger army if positioned wisely and driven by a strong will. When you think about heroic moments in history, remember Bastogne. Picture the snow-covered foxholes, the paratroopers sharing meager scraps of food, the booming artillery, and General McAuliffe's defiant one-word reply. Through those images, you'll see why these soldiers and their story continue to inspire decades later.

Like many World War II stories, the Siege of Bastogne shows us the power of determination. The men of the 101st Airborne weren't superheroes—they felt cold, hunger, and fear. Yet they refused to let despair take over. By working together, trusting their leaders, and leaning on each other's strength, they endured a terrifying situation. Their unwavering stand reminds us that courage doesn't always mean charging forward. Sometimes, it means holding your ground when everything around you says to give up. For the 101st Airborne in Bastogne, that courage became their lasting legacy—showing the world how a determined few can help safeguard freedom for many.

Step into the storm of battle! Scan to view colorized footage of the 101st Airborne's stand at Bastogne

Afterword

As we conclude our journey through these inspiring tales of World War II, let's take a moment to celebrate the triumph of the human spirit. Across every story we've explored, ordinary men and women rose above fear and adversity. They faced the harsh realities of war and still chose courage and integrity. Even in the darkest times, hope thrived because individuals acted bravely. They showed us that light can shine through the darkest clouds.

Throughout these stories, unity and collaboration emerge as powerful themes. Many acts of heroism came from camaraderie. Diverse groups of soldiers fought side by side, forming bonds that transcended backgrounds. Civilians, too, banded together to rescue strangers. They showed us that unity, not division, leads to the greatest victories. Together, they saved countless lives.

Innovation and adaptability also played significant roles. People had to think creatively to overcome obstacles. From codebreakers to inflatable tanks, from nighttime missions in biplanes to crafting life-saving visas, World War II pushed the limits of human ingenuity. These inventive strategies remind us that the human mind can find solutions even when the stakes are high.

Compassion shone brightly during these trying times. Empathy became a powerful weapon. People risked everything to protect the vulnerable, shield the persecuted, and lift the spirits of their comrades. Acts of kindness, both big and small, emerged as beacons of hope against the cruelty of war. They showed that even in the toughest times, compassion can prevail.

The lessons from these stories are not just history. They are enduring messages for future generations. True heroism often lies in small but decisive moral choices. These are moments when individuals refuse to give in to despair or hate. We must remember these stories as ongoing inspirations. They guide us in how we can act in today's conflicts or crises.

As we part, let's end on a powerful note: From terrible tragedy, the best of human endeavor can indeed surface. Courage, hope, and unity have the power to reshape the darkest chapters of humanity. They can turn them into stories that inspire for generations to come.

You, as a reader, are part of this legacy. The tales you have read are not just tales of the past. They are lessons for us all. As people who believe deeply in helping kids understand history, we hope these stories inspire you. We hope they remind you that you can make a difference. Whether big or small, your actions always matter.

So, take these stories with you. Share them. Let them inspire you and others to stand up for what is right. Let them guide you in your choices. Together, we can create a world where courage, hope, and unity continue to light our way.

Endnotes

The quotes featured in this book have been slightly adjusted for storytelling and entertainment purposes, yet they are based on documented historical events and biographical research. While we strive to maintain accuracy and authenticity, some dialogue and details may vary from original accounts.

www.ingramcontent.com/pod-product-compliance
Lightning Source LLC
Chambersburg PA
CBHW072210070526
44585CB00015B/1282